David Lewis is a research psychologist with a special interest in the effects of the emotions on intellectual attainment. He is a director of Action on Phobias, a charity which he helped set up in order to provide help for phobic suffers. He is also involved in helping children think more effectively through a special home-based training programme which he developed for Children Unlimited. Currently more than a thousand families are working with his methods. His books on child development have been published in more than thirty countries. He lectures widely and is a frequent broadcaster. At present he is carrying out research at the University of Sussex.

James Greene is a psychologist whose professional interests are centred on personality theory and testing. He has carried out considerable research on the examination and analysis of drawings to uncover hidden aspects of temperament and ability in children and adults. He has a Master's degree in psychology and a postgraduate qualification in psychological assessment.

Apart from his academic activities, James Greene works as a consultant to industry, advising companies in the use of psychological methods in personnel selection and training. During the last few years, he has also coauthored several books (with David Lewis) on popular psychological topics. These have appeared in the UK, the USA, and a number of other countries.

Your Child's Drawings ... Their Hidden Meaning

David Lewis and James Greene

Hutchinson

London   Melbourne   Sydney   Auckland   Johannesburg

Hutchinson & Co. (Publishers) Ltd
An imprint of the Hutchinson Publishing Group

17–21 Conway Street, London w1p 6jd

Hutchinson Group (Australia) Pty Ltd
30–32 Cremorne Street, Richmond South, Victoria 3121
po Box 151, Broadway, New South Wales 2007

Hutchinson Group (nz) Ltd
32–34 View Road, po Box 40-086, Glenfield, Auckland 10

Hutchinson Group (sa) Pty Ltd
po Box 337, Bergvlei 2012, South Africa

First published 1983
© David Lewis and James Greene 1983

Set in Century Schoolbook
by Tradespools Ltd, Frome, Somerset

Printed in Great Britain by The Anchor Press Ltd and
bound by Wm Brendon & Son Ltd both of Tiptree, Essex.
British Library Cataloguing in Publication Data

Lewis, David
    Your child's drawings.
    1. Interpersonal communication in children
    I. Title   II. Greene, James
    155.4'18   BF723.C57

ISBN 0 09 151330 8 (cased)
ISBN 0 09 151331 6 (paper)

Contents

CHAPTER ONE

What your child's pictures really reveal

Your child's pictures can tell you much more about him or her than words. With each stroke of the pencil and every sweep of the brush children create not simply images of the world around them, but intimate and revealing self-portraits.

A child's choice of subjects, preference for a particular colour, use of space and shading, the speed with which drawings are made and the skill shown when applying paint, the way images are positioned on the page or lines are drawn, the details they decide to include or prefer to leave out are just a few of the keys that enable parents, teachers and all concerned with the wellbeing of young children to unlock some of childhood's most closely guarded secrets.

Once you have learned to identify the signals and interpret the hidden language of pictures it becomes possible to understand a child's dreams and fears, hopes and despairs, conflicts and confusions clearly and comprehensively. Our purpose in writing this book is to explain how to analyse any sort of children's art, from casual scribbles to painstakingly detailed paintings, before using your new insights to provide guidance and effective help.

By mastering the art of picture assessment you will be able to:

Identify key personality factors and understand their influence in shaping a child's attitudes and actions.

Explore the child's feelings, as revealed by their choice of colours, and assess their emotional health.

Monitor a child's anxiety and pinpoint the reasons why fears may have arisen.

Examine friendships to find out whether a child is experiencing any social problems.

Investigate a child's impulsivity in order to discover its effect on behaviour at home and achievement in class.

Assess creativity and see whether you need to enhance the child's powers of imagination. Measure intellectual development to learn whether a child's true mental potential is being realized.

As psychologists dealing with the upsets and problems of childhood on an almost daily basis, we have long been impressed by how well pictures provide a window through which one can observe the child's innermost thoughts and feelings. We use the analysis of drawings and paintings as an invaluable aid to assessing children and discovering the cause of their difficulties.

Here is just one of many case histories which well illustrates how pictures speak louder than words:

Not long ago, we were asked to help a ten-year-old boy called John whose behaviour was causing his parents great concern. When they first came to see us and described John's behaviour, it was quite hard to picture the small, slightly built boy with his unruly, dark brown hair and watchful, wary expression as a pint-sized Attila. Yet that was the role in which John was being cast by his mother, Mary, and stepfather Arthur. And, as the list of John's misdeeds grew longer and longer, they certainly offered reason enough for parental complaint.

John was prone to frequent temper tantrums during which no piece of breakable property was safe. Toys, ornaments, crockery – on one occasion even a window – were vandalized during his outbursts. His fury exploded over the most trivial incidents and, we were assured, seemed utterly unpredictable. Between rages the boy was withdrawn and moody. He would never speak to his stepfather unless asked a direct question and had recently begun to reject his mother as well.

He fought with his stepbrother Jonathan who, being two years older, taller and a lot stronger, usually gave him a hiding. He quarrelled bitterly with stepsister Samantha, a year his junior, and sometimes hit her. Although this usually led to a spanking from his stepfather, the repeated punishments did nothing to change the boy's behaviour. John had taken to wetting his bed, to crying for no apparent reason and – on a number of occasions – to playing truant from school. By no stretch of the imagination, then, could John be described as a happy child.

Throughout their detailed, and at times bitter, account of his conduct, the boy sat silent and almost motionless, eyes fixed on his feet. When asked, by us, for some comment he simply shrugged or mumbled, scuffing his feet on the carpet. 'He's only recently been this way,' Mary explained sadly. 'Up to a few months ago he was so good, such a happy boy. I just can't understand why he should have turned out this way.'

On their next visit, we asked Mary to bring in as many of John's paintings and drawings as she could find. Of special interest to us, we emphasized, were pictures showing the whole family. By going through drawers and cupboards, and asking John's form teacher, Mary managed to bring in more than a dozen. One of them, painted around February of that year is shown in illustration 1 of the colour section.

The picture immediately told us a great deal about John, and his family. It confirmed that, at the start of the year, he had been an outgoing, happy child, perhaps more emotional than most, but growing towards greater maturity and self-reliance – although evidence of conflict and signs of hostility were also present. John pictured feelings of isolation from his step-brother and stepsister, the older boy being seen as especially hostile. Arthur was regarded as dominating the family, while John's drawing of his mother revealed that he felt closer to her, and liked her better, than anybody else in the family. Anxiety, mild but unmistakable, was also hinted at, and even though John seems to have been happy at this time the portrait he created was not one of a warm and loving family.

During subsequent family visits, we spent some time talking to Arthur and Mary while John was shown into a quiet playroom, provided with large sheets of paper and a wide range of paints and asked to produce pictures showing his family. One of his earliest paintings is in illustration 2 of the colour section. John indentified himself as the small boy in blue kneeling in front of his mother. Samantha stands behind Mary, while Arthur is clearly giving some instruction to the family, and Jonathan is at the extreme right of the picture.

The dominant themes of the picture are hostility, aggression and a sense of isolation. However, John's painting expresses not only anger but also considerable anxiety. It is the creation of a child who feels helpless in the face of an almost over-whelming personal tragedy. The attachment to his mother, suggested in the first picture, has now disappeared. He appears to consider the whole family to be against him, especially his stepfather. Yet there are also some indications that John would like to control his outbursts and welcomes the approval of adults.

The family was in therapy throughout the summer and autumn. John was asked to draw or paint portraits of his family or of individuals at regular intervals, and these were used both as a talking point during private discussions with him and as a way of observing changes in his attitudes and emotions. Although he slowly became more forthcoming when seen alone, he could not describe his emotions in any detail or express feelings about other members of the family. Fortunately, his pictures proved more communicative. They spoke for the unhappy ten-year-old, telling us many of the things he probably longed to say aloud.

In November, John painted the picture shown in illustration 3 of the colour section. Its mood is one of almost Wagnerian gloom. The sense of unhappiness is profound. John now feels utterly isolated from everybody else in the family. Arthur's dominance seems even greater. His mother has rejected him entirely. He plays alone in the garden under a lowering, alien sun. The dominant colours are black and purple with red, overpainted in places, completing the dramatic effect. Here we see guilt, depression, isolation, fear and anxiety. John is a child torn by conflict and locked in misery. Yet, surprisingly perhaps, the picture contains some hopeful signs. The boy feels less helpless. He is less fearful. There is a growing sense of self-reliance. As he approaches his eleventh birthday, John seems to be coming to terms with his crisis. Around this time, too, John's aggressive behaviour, which had gradually been declining, disappeared completely. Now he was withdrawn and emotionally cold. He rejected affectionate advances from Mary and remained aloof from his stepfather.

The story does have a happy ending, however. The family's problems were gradually solved. They slowly came closer to one another. John's sense of isolation began to disappear. Some fifteen months after therapy began, John's behaviour was no longer causing them any concern.

In June he painted the picture in illustration 4 of the colour section. Clearly they are a far more united family and John, standing beside his mother, feels himself accepted again. His painting reveals him to be much happier, although still dependent and rather emotional. His stepfather's dominance has declined (in therapy Mary was encouraged to be more assertive) and the boy seems to have gone a long way towards accepting him, although he is still much closer to his mother.

What is the family history behind the boy's problems?

John's father was killed in a road accident when he was four, and for the next five years Mary brought up her son unaided. She then married Arthur, a widower ten years her senior, who already had two children of his own. To Mary's relief, John seemed to accept her marriage, and for nearly a year all went reasonably well. Arthur was then made redundant from his work in the accounts department of a textile factory and, although he was lucky enough to find fresh employment after only a couple of months out of work, the experience left him deeply depressed. He started drinking, not heavily but enough to make him edgy and irritable. His frustrations were vented largely on John, although Mary also came in for verbal assault if she attempted to defend her son.

The boy often found his mother crying and, quite reasonably, blamed his stepfather for her distress. Arthur's children tended to take their father's side.

At about the same time Arthur began an affair with a

woman in his office and left to set up home with her. He was away for less than five weeks before she ended the relationship, and Arthur returned home. Although John had taken his stepfather's departure without any obvious sign of emotion, other than relief, his return provoked the first of many violent temper tantrums. At first Mary defended him and blamed Arthur for the boy's behaviour. But, slowly, she lost patience with the boy and began to see him as part of the reason why her marriage was so unhappy. At this point John's behaviour had become so intolerable that his parents sought professional guidance.

As you read on, you will discover how to read those same revealing messages in John's pictures. We suggest that you return to the pictures at the end of each assessment chapter to see how many of the key signs you can now identify and interpret. As a guide, you will be looking out for the following:

Colour choice (The colours shown in our illustrations dominated 75 per cent of John's paintings.)

Overpainting (another regular feature of paintings produced in the autumn and winter)

Angles and straight lines used in place of curves

Distortions and omissions in human figures

Grouping of figures

Posture and gesture

Presence of the sun (this occurred in 90 per cent of John's drawings)

Amount of detail present

We have chosen John's story to illustrate the power of picture analysis, because his paintings offer such an interesting and detailed example of the ways in which a child's most profound emotions find clear expression in their art. A child's thoughts and feelings need not be so intense, however, nor their behaviour anywhere near as dramatic, for pictures to provide us with important and fascinating insights.

We are mainly concerned with children aged between 5 and

12, young children whose drawings and paintings are not so much expressions of creative talent as symbolic representations of their personal view of the world. Simply because they are symbolic, they possess the power to tell us things that the child may be unwilling, or unable, to put into words.

The story of children's paintings is, in a real sense, the tale of mankind's earliest involvement with art. Its roots lie not in the nursery nor the art class, but deep beneath the earth in the labyrinthine caverns that were man's first art galleries.

Why pictures reveal so much

On a fine afternoon, in 1879, the Marquis de Sautuola and his five-year-old daughter climbed a steep hill outside the Spanish village of Santillana del Mar in the province of Cantabria. A short time earlier, men digging out a nearby quarry during a hunt had stumbled on a series of deep caves. Now, with nothing better to do with his time, the Marquis decided to amuse himself by searching the floor of the Altamira caves for bones and Stone Age implements.

While her father hunted for trophies, the little girl wandered away into a part of the cave so low that only a small child could stand upright. Suddenly the unsteady light from her candle flickered across the roof of the cave and she cried out in surprise and delight 'Toros! Toros!'

What had caught the child's astonished gaze was an exquisite painting of bison – the now famous Altamira frescoes – some of the earliest examples of human art ever discovered. More than 2000 BC, Stone Age hunters had first painstakingly engraved those creatures on the cave roof, using sharp flint tools called burins, before adding brilliant colours made from mineral dyes, iron oxides to produce different shades of red, carbonates of iron for colours ranging from yellow to dark orange, with burnt bones providing the black. They had mixed their colours with animal fats, using paint tubes and palettes fashioned from bones. Deep in the caves of Spain and France they then created their paintings, a frieze of horses or reindeer, cattle and herdsmen, working by the guttering light of a moss wick burning on animal fats within a container fashioned from a human skull.

That a child should have been the first person to view those paintings in more than thirty centuries was entirely appropriate, for her vision of the world was probably far closer to that of the Palaeolithic craftsmen who had created them than any contemporary adult's could have been.

Stone Age artists invested time and effort in their paintings, not from any desire to brighten up their drab cave homes – these pictures are hidden in the depths of mountains where men never lived – but as a form of ritual magic. By drawing the beasts on whom survival depended, they hoped to ensure the success of their hunting and the health of their herds. The line and form of the images created, their position within the overall picture, the detail included, the colours chosen and the scenes depicted had a deep symbolic significance for them. They were used to express feelings about themselves and about their world at a depth and with an intensity that lay beyond the reach of any other form of communication. Pictures took the place of the linguistic skills primitive man lacked, as they still do in the art of a young child.

Before a child has fully mastered the use of spoken language, it is only natural that spontaneous images should provide the most powerful means of self-expression. Yet, even when he or she has achieved an adult skill and fluency with words, drawings and paintings can still prove more satisfying and satisfactory than the spoken word in portraying deeper thoughts and feelings.

Palaeolithic artists dreaming of successful hunts and easy kills scratched at the walls of their gloomy caves with flints, hoping that dreams might become reality through the magical power of pictures. For young children, too, pencil, brush and paper often are the means of expressing their fondest hopes and most profound fears. If children feel that important elements are missing from their life, or when they feel denied of love or deprived of attention, friendless or a failure, angry or anxious, then these sentiments are likely to be expressed, either directly or in a disguised form, in the pictures they create.

Feelings that a child is unwilling, or unable, to put into words can often be expressed more easily through drawings and paintings. Emotions too powerful or too confusing to think about clearly can find release through the use of paint on paper. Relationships which arouse such strong feelings of love or hate that a child is unable to find the right words to describe them may be vividly portrayed in a drawing or painting. In short, pictures can speak with ease when the child is lost for words.

How picture analysis will help you

When we talk to parents and teachers about picture analysis, two questions are frequently asked. The first is if such assessments are really necessary in order to understand children properly. The second is whether it is valid to use their drawings and paintings in this way.

To the first question, one can certainly argue that caring parents already know all they need to about a child's personality, emotions, creative talents, social skills and intellectual abilities simply through everyday observation. Others, however, may be less perceptive. More importantly, however, even within the most affectionate relationships, problems can still arise. A child's behaviour can suddenly become difficult to understand and, perhaps, to tolerate.

A previously happy-go-lucky youngster becomes moody and withdrawn, a once self-confident child grows increasingly dependent and clinging, a bright pupil begins to fall behind the rest of the class, an easy-going boy or girl becomes increasingly aggressive. Children who once made friends easily grow more and more isolated, those who used to take setbacks calmly start reacting to failure with tears and temper tantrums.

Sometimes it seems to happen almost overnight, as family relationships, once warm, open and trusting, are put in jeopardy, friendships are lost and classroom performance declines. At such times parents often say despairingly: 'But we were always so close ... how could he have felt that way for so long without our ever realizing it?' Sometimes they are angry with the child, more often they feel guilty over what has happened, but uncertain how best to put matters right because they still do not really know what went wrong in the first place.

The root cause of the family's difficulties can often be found

in the parents' misunderstanding of their child's true character. Such mistakes usually arise for one of two reasons: either
the adult is not sufficiently involved with the child or – a more
frequent cause of error – they are too close to them emotionally. To love somebody deeply is to see them in a very special
kind of way. It is only natural to be slightly blind to their less
attractive qualities while being well aware of their good
features. Since there are both positive and negative aspects to
personality and emotions, this unintended bias can focus
parental attention on their child's strong points while playing
down less desirable features.

While parents are usually so close to their children that
their judgements may be at fault, teachers with a busy
schedule and large numbers of children to attend to may fail
because they are never close enough to any individual child.
This is especially true, in our experience, of pupils considered
to be particularly troublesome. It is, of course, just these
youngsters who are most likely to need the greatest understanding and the clearest guidance.

Picture analysis allows even the busiest adults to assess
children quickly but accurately and to monitor their emotional
health and social wellbeing over a period of time. It enables
parents to stand back from their children and so obtain a better
perspective on their character and conduct. The one valid
reason for assessing a child in this way is to provide the best
advice and guidance, in the most effective manner and at the
most appropriate time.

The danger of assessing children at all lies in the risk of
creating a self-fulfilling prophecy of success or failure, happiness or distress. A chilling example of such a prophecy at work
comes from an American study of very young children in a
New York nursery school. Researchers discovered that, within
a fortnight of their arrival at the school, the head teacher had
placed her small charges at one of three tables. There was her
'success' table, her 'middle of the road' table, and her 'failures'
table. She made her assessments entirely subjectively,
categorizing the children on the basis of their family backgrounds, manners, conversational ability and the way they
were dressed.

When they carried out their own objective assessments, the

investigators discovered that the teacher's system was completely ineffective. There were some bright children on the 'failures' table and several less able youngsters on the 'success' table. When they returned to reassess the same children a few years later, however, this more or less random distribution had changed significantly. Now all the youngsters seated at the 'success' table were doing better than their companions while those on the 'failures' table were doing far worse than average. By labelling children in a certain way their futures had been not only prejudged but virtually preordained.

Assessments should never be used as the first step in categorizing or ranking children according to their supposed aptitudes, attitudes and abilities. Harmful enough when applied to adults, such pigeonholing can have a devastating effect on the child. This book is about assessing children in order to help them: it is intended to replace subjective impressions with reliable and objective understanding. It is only through such knowledge that effective help and guidance can be provided.

How to use the book

We begin by looking at aspects of the child's personality, since these factors exert an important and powerful influence over almost everything else the child thinks or feels.

After describing how to assess these factors, we explain how best to build on personality strengths while minimizing their less positive features. From personality we move to emotions, and show you how picture analysis can provide clear insights into both passing moods and more lasting responses. Chapter 6 explores the powerful emotions of anxiety and depression, considers the kind of crisis which can crop up in a child's life and offers a number of practical procedures for helping to resolve such problems. In Chapter 7 you will be shown how to assess your child's friendships and feelings about other members of the family. If any failures in relationships are detected, Chapter 8 will provide helpful guidance. Chapter 9 considers the role of temperament and its effects on a child's behaviour and attainments.

Creativity and procedures for enhancing the child's imagination are dealt with in Chapter 10, while Chapter 11 explains how to assess a child's intellectual development using a drawing test. Finally, in Chapter 12, we will consider how the information you have gained can be put to the best possible use.

The first assessment

This is designed to help you get an idea of how drawing tests can be used and to appreciate the amount of information which even a simple assessment provides. The illustration on pages 20 and 21 shows 16 designs which your child should copy, from memory, on to a single sheet of white, unlined, A4 size paper. Start by copying them yourself, so they occupy one side of an A4 sheet.

When you have done this, explain what you want your child to do, saying something along these lines. 'I've got a game here to see how good you are at remembering drawings. In a moment I will show you some pictures, one at a time. Look at each of them for a few seconds, and then draw them on this sheet of paper. There are 16 drawings and I want you to fit all of them on to one side of the paper. Do you understand?'

Once you are certain your child knows what is wanted, show him or her the sheet and point to the first design. Allow the child five or six seconds to study it, then turn the sheet face down and ask for the copy to be drawn. Do not prompt the child in any way, or allow any drawing to start until you have covered up the designs.

You will tell your child the test is to assess memory to disguise its real purpose: this small subterfuge is necessary because if the truth is known before the assessment is completed, the result will be unreliable. What you are really interested in finding out is how well your child has *organized* all 16 designs on that single sheet of paper.

Count out eight of the designs, across the page, and cut the paper at this point to produce two pieces with eight copies on each. Place the smaller portion on top of the larger and use a ruler to measure the difference between them. If the designs have been laid out in such a way that it was impossible to produce a straight cut, do not worry. Just take the distance at two or three points and average the result. The larger the difference, the less efficiently the child has laid out the designs and the less planning has gone into the task.

Age of Child	Score	Score Range
4– 6	Low	< 7
	High	> 7
7– 8	Low	< 5
	High	> 5
9–10	Low	< 3
	High	> 3
10+	Low	< 2
	High	> 2

Studies by Professor Raymond Cattell, at the University of Hawaii, from whose original research we have developed this test, have shown that children in the low score range tend to behave quite differently from those in the high score range. The higher or lower your child's score within either range, the more closely their approach to life is likely to match the tendencies described below.

High-score range

These children tend to be less self-reliant and more timid than youngsters of the same age. They rely on help, reassurance and encouragement from parents and teachers and become uncertain and unhappy if left too much to their own devices.

They seldom organize their time very efficiently and make careless mistakes in schoolwork.

Because they have difficulty in making precise and accurately co-ordinated movements high-scoring youngsters are frequently poor at sports, somewhat accident-prone in play and generally untidy when writing, drawing or attempting any type of task demanding fine attention to detail.

They are likely to show the greatest interest in and do best at subjects such as art, history and the humanities. They will be less interested in science, engineering and mathematics.

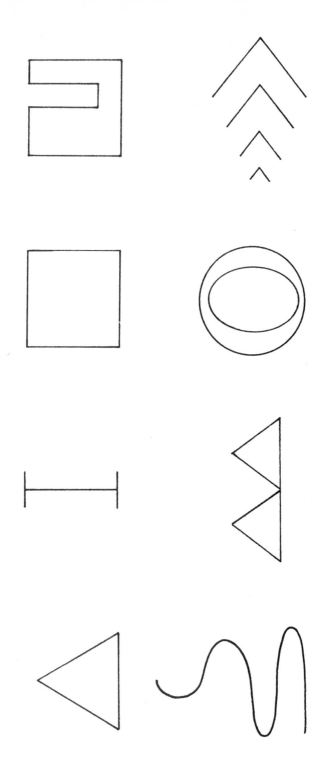

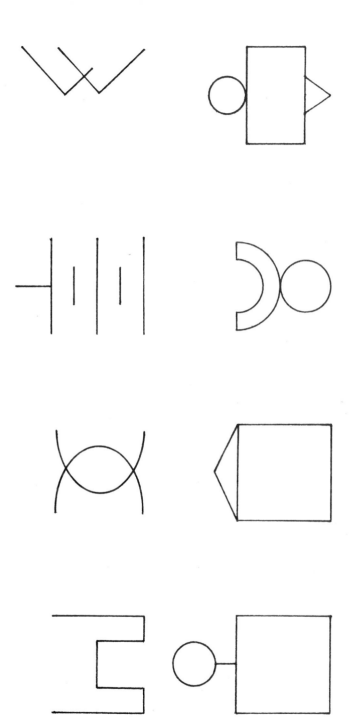

ILLUSTRATION 1 Copy or trace these diagrams onto one A4 sized sheet of paper

When dealing with this type of child remember their emotional vulnerability and try to avoid remarks calculated to hurt their feelings. Comments which a less sensitive child would simply shrug off can cause far more distress than intended. You will find further advice on helping such children in Chapter 4.

Low-score range

These children tend to be more independent, assured and self-confident than most. They may be unusually optimistic about their prospects of success in life, even though the goals they set themselves are frequently ambitious.

They are rather impatient, easily irritated and likely to have fewer close friendships than high scorers. Seldom shy, they will talk about themselves freely and frankly.

They show considerable enthusiasm for new ideas and projects. Unlike high scorers, they are not overly sensitive and can take criticism in their stride.

The interests of low-scoring children are more likely to lie in science and technology, engineering, mathematics, economics and business studies. They make good use of their intelligence, often pushing themselves to their intellectual limits.

Their tough, no-nonsense approach to life makes some people regard them as unfeeling or emotionally cold. They are generally assertive and prepared to stand up for themselves in an argument.

We have provided these thumbnail sketches to illustrate how much information can be gained from simple drawing tests. You may feel that what we have said is a fair description of your child's attitudes; this is most likely to be true if their scores were towards the upper or lower limits of each score range. You should not, however, regard those comments – however appropriate – as being a definitive summary of the child's personality and prospects. Instead, keep these comments in mind as you begin to master picture analysis, which can be used to paint a complete portrait of the child by bringing together the information provided by the assessments.

How picture analysis helps

The major advantages which picture analysis offers over other ways of assessing and understanding children can be summarized as follows:

The results are very reliable. Research around the world has shown that these interpretations are among the most accurate obtained through any means of assessment.

Children enjoy doing the tests because they seem like just another game. While many youngsters dislike having to answer questions about themselves, and often give misleading answers so as to make a 'good impression', drawing tests are completed quickly, easily and enjoyably. Furthermore, the results cannot be faked or modified.

The techniques of analysis are so easy to learn and take so little time to carry out that you can use them almost immediately to gain a greater understanding of your child's attitudes and abilities. They can also be employed on a day-to-day basis for monitoring behaviour and keeping a watchful eye on feelings.

They are sensitive to the most subtle shifts of mood, as an experiment carried out by Dr Reiner Kraus, one of Germany's leading child psychologists, clearly showed:

He asked a group of ten and eleven-year-olds to draw lines expressing various emotional states. Some drew 'sad' lines, others 'happy' ones. There were 'angry' lines and 'anxious' lines, 'embarrassed' lines and 'joyous' lines. Dr Kraus then showed these drawings to a second group of children and asked them to say what sort of emotions they felt were being depicted. Remarkably, more than 70 per cent of the second group's assessments were correct.

The revealing power of pictures offers adults a rare chance to explore the world of their children. To see life through their eyes, to share their feelings, catch their moods and understand their emotions. It is one of the most exciting and rewarding journeys that any adult who cares about children can ever make.

CHAPTER TWO

Making a Start

The procedures for analysing children's drawings described in the following chapters are based on our own research and professional experiences as clinical and educational psychologists, as well as on the work of other research psychologists, child development experts and specialists in the field of education.

During these studies, which have been carried out at European, American, and Far Eastern universities, investigators used a wide range of sophisticated techniques to identify key features, interpret their significance and ensure that the conclusions they obtained were both accurate and consistent. Now that this work has been carried out, however, there is no need for any complex or costly equipment in order to carry out a successful analysis of children's drawings. You can make use of all the assessment procedures we describe with little difficulty and a minimum of equipment. Virtually everything necessary can be found around most people's homes.

Equipping yourself for picture analysis

Although some pictures will obviously be more revealing than others, it is possible to analyse drawings and paintings produced in any type of medium. It makes no difference whether they are drawn with lead pencils or felt-tipped pens, ballpoint pens or brushes, sticks of chalk or pieces of charcoal. They can be black or white sketches or brightly coloured with poster paints or oils, water colour or crayons, inks or aerosol spray cans.

Our only reservation concerns the assessment of a child's emotions by means of coloured images (see Chapter 5). Here it is obviously essential to ensure that a full range of colours – not merely a few of the primary ones – is available as the crucial aspect of this assessment is colour preference. Some of the drawing tests in the book are scored by making comparisons with examples printed in the appropriate chapter. In these cases you may find comparison easier if your child completes the assessments in fibre pen or ballpoint pen.

Choosing the paper
Your first choice should be good quality, white, unlined paper. White paper makes it easy to study the rhythm and stroke of the drawings; while unlined paper is preferable because printed lines will influence the way your child creates a particular drawing and the relative size of objects within the drawing. In some drawing tests both these factors are significant. Although in most instances paper size is unimportant, you will find a couple in which A4 sized paper is specified: this is because, when we were carrying out the research from which that particular scoring system was developed, this format was adopted. If larger or smaller paper is used, the results will no longer be accurate.

Sheets of 25 × 20 cm (10 × 8 in) or larger are preferable, since smaller areas tend to cramp the natural drawing style. So far as paper *thickness* is concerned, a medium weight is best. One important technique involves assessing the pressure of the drawing strokes by feeling the extent of indentation on the paper. It cannot, therefore, be carried out on very thick cartridge paper. On the other hand, if the paper is too thin and flimsy, the child may have difficulty in handling it, and the frustration this produces may bias your results. When analysing a child's spontaneous pictures, however, the type of paper used is unimportant and the work may be created on anything from thick card to tissue paper.

If you intend to monitor your child's drawings on a weekly or monthly basis, a very helpful approach on occasions, then an artist's sketchpad containing unlined white paper offers the most practical approach. Even when assessing only your own child it is helpful to identify each picture with the artist's name and the date it was produced. When you look back over a large number of drawings and paintings, in order perhaps to identify the point at which changes in emotions or relationships took place, it is easy to become confused about the order in which they were created, or even the child responsible for a particular picture. Accurate record-keeping is, of course, essential if you are assessing a large number of children.

Magnifying-glass
Although most of the judgments you will be making can be done using the naked eye, it is sometimes helpful to have a large × 3 magnifying-glass. It is sometimes possible to identify details with a lens that might otherwise have gone unobserved.

Ruler
A transparent ruler is required for certain assessment procedures in which it is necessary to measure the areas occupied by a particular image or to compare the size of different parts of the picture.

Watch
A watch or clock with a digital read-out with a second hand will be needed for some of the tests which must be timed to the nearest second.

Analysis in action

While research has shown that picture analysis is one of the more reliable forms of psychological assessment available, no technique for assessing another human being is ever 100 per cent accurate. Like everything else in science, *psychometrics* – the application of measurement and mathematics to psychological testing – deals not with certainties but with probabilities. Any test result tells you, therefore, that one interpretation is far more likely to be correct than any other. To be scientifically acceptable, this probability must usually be at least 1 in 20, and preferably far higher. In other words, the result of a particular assessment means that it will be right in the vast majority of cases and incorrect only 5 times out of 100, or less. Use your new knowledge to guide your understanding of the child and as a means of helping to create the kind of surroundings in which they can feel most secure and prove most successful. Never look on it as a final or definitive statement about their attitudes, aptitudes and abilities.

View all your child's pictures as objectively as possible, making a positive effort not to be biased by the intimacy of your relationship. Try to assess the work through the eyes of a stranger. This is especially important if the results seem to confirm your previous judgments. Make quite certain that the features you judge to be present in the paintings or drawings really exist on the paper and not just in your imagination. If in doubt get a friend to read the appropriate chapter and assess the picture without mentioning the results of your own analysis; see how many points of agreement – and disagreement – result.

Different features are dealt with under a number of chapter headings, with various key features and signs separated into appropriate sections for easy reading and clear understanding. When assessing your child's drawings and paintings, however, you must integrate all your knowledge to produce an overall view of their personality, emotions, social relationships, intellectual aptitudes and creative talents. Bear in mind the following points:

Avoid focusing your attention on just one or two points or you may unintentionally overlook or misinterpret significant features. Do not decide to ignore certain characteristics because they fail to fit in with previous conclusions.

Make certain that you explore each and every aspect of the picture, reserving final judgment until all the tests we describe have been carried out.

Do not be in too much of a hurry to do this. There are many enjoyable projects and you should make certain your child remains interested and highly motivated by spacing them sensibly over a period of days or weeks.

Keep all the drawing sessions relaxed so that your child looks forward to them and continues to regard them as a game.

Before assessing your own children you may find it helpful to practise by analysing the pictures of a child you know only casually. This will allow you to perfect your assessment skills without the risk of subjective feelings getting in the way. If you do decide to do this, however, it is essential to be extremely tactful – and very cautious – when presenting your findings to the child's parents. Ideally, you should get them to read the book and carry out their own analysis before exchanging notes.

Remember, too, that all the features we describe, whether dealing with personality factors, emotions, relationships or intellectual abilities, have both positive and negative features to them. Instead of dwelling on any problems you may have found – or concentrating only on the plus side of the analysis – try to integrate all aspects of the assessment. Unless you do this the report is going to sound either unconvincing or overly harsh. Always remember the only valid reason for assessing children – no matter what technique is employed – is to gain the deep understanding essential if one is to offer the most appropriate help and guidance.

Imagine that you have worked through the book, carried out a number of the special tests and now have several drawings and paintings awaiting detailed analysis. To ensure that each analysis is carried out in an organized and systematic manner, we have developed a technique called *Funnel Analysis*, so named because the approach requires you to work from the general to the particular (see Diagram 1 on the next page). This enables you to approach each new picture with a clear idea about how to start the assessment and how to continue with your analysis until every detail of significance has been identified and all the information extracted from the images.

Funnel analysis in action

In the first stage (box 1 in Diagram 1) you pay attention to the picture's *Overall appearance*, by looking at such features as:

The child's choice of subject (unless this was dictated by somebody else)

The dominant colour (where a free choice from a wide range of possible colours was available)

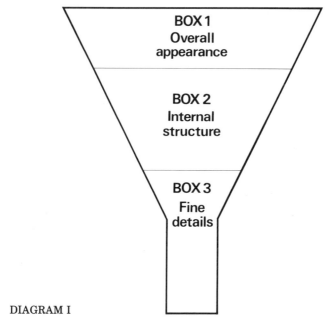

DIAGRAM I

How much of the available space the picture occupies

Whether it fills the entire sheet or whether it has been confined to just a small part of the paper

The general impression you get from looking at this picture

The degree of skill and care that has gone into its creation

Having established an over-view of the picture, you then study its *Internal Structure* (see box 2). This is a crucial stage in the assessment since many of your most interesting findings will be made at this level of analysis. Here you will be looking at the way the child has placed objects or human figures within the composition:

Are they close together or at some distance? Do one or two of them appear to have been deliberately isolated from the remainder?

Consider the relative sizes of the figures – does one seem to dominate the group?

Look at posture and stance – is one person standing up while the others are seated? If the child has included himself/herself in the scene how prominent is he/she? Has he/she been pictured as part of a group or well separated from the rest?

Examine the way the drawing has been made. Are there mainly straight lines and angles in places where one might have expected smooth curves?

Has the child used shading and white spaces to produce a more subtle image?

Are parts of any human figures omitted or distorted?

Finally, move down to the last part of the funnel (see box 3) and consider the picture's *Fine details*. These can be likened to fingerprints since they will include small but significant features which give your child's pictures their individuality.

Look at faces and note the attention paid to their features. How much time and trouble has been expended in drawing the eyes, nose and mouth? Do the eyes have pupils and the nose nostrils? Are there eyebrows and eyelashes? Have the lips been formed with care or was the child content with an approximate line to indicate the position of the mouth? Is hair drawn in or just indicated by a scribble or splash of colour? Are there minor blemishes like spots or freckles? Is the person smoking a pipe or cigarette? Are they wearing glasses?

Do clothes include such details as buttons and buckles, belts or braces? Are there pockets in suits and pleats in skirts? Do shoes come complete with laces? Is any jewellery included?

Clearly, the skill with which the pictures are drawn and painted will vary according to the child's age and artistic talents. When carrying out this analysis you are not concerned about *how well* these details are represented, only whether or not any attempt has been made to include them. By the time you have reached this point of the analysis you should have obtained many clear and fascinating insights into the mind of the child.

CHAPTER THREE

How pictures reveal personality

Personality shapes your child's future by providing the building blocks from which intellectual abilities, social skills and emotional responses are formed. Its inborn factors determine whether children will be outgoing or inward-looking, sociable or solitary, dependent or self-sufficient, anxious or assertive, confident or uncertain. Research has also shown that personality plays a vital role in such crucial aspects of intelligence as the ability to concentrate, persistence in the face of setbacks, the speed and accuracy with which new knowledge is mastered and the amount of effort expended when tackling complex or unfamiliar tasks.

A child's vulnerability to emotional problems, together with the type, intensity and duration of such difficulties is also significantly affected by personality factors. Although psychologists are still not sure exactly how many of these factors there are, we have found that one can usefully explore five of them when looking for ways of understanding and helping children.

Making the assessments

Because it will be easier to remain objective if you are unaware, for the moment, of the precise nature of the personality factors being assessed, we suggest that you carry out your observations and tests before reading the next chapter.

At all times, keep in mind the importance of turning each session into a game so that the child really enjoys doing the drawing tests and looks forward to doing some more. Do not try to complete all five assessments at the same time, but spread them over at least as many days.

Factor one

Copy the designs in illustration 1 on to a sheet of plain paper. While there is no need to reproduce them exactly, be careful to retain the same general shape. Show these to your child saying something along these lines:
'You see these shapes I've drawn? I want you to finish the pictures for me by joining up the lines so as to get rid of all the gaps. You can do this in any way you like.' It may be helpful, especially with younger children, to demonstrate exactly what is required by completing one of the designs. The dotted lines in illustration 2 show some of the many ways this might be accomplished. We have provided one extra design (only ten are to be completed) for demonstration purposes where necessary.

When your child has finished the task, point to the first and say:
'Look at this drawing, think about it for a moment, and then tell me if it reminds you of anything.' If, after a few moments' reflection, your child is unable to see anything in the first design, move to the second and repeat your question. When a shape does remind your child of something award that design 1 point. The actual answer is unimportant, and there is no need to keep a note of it. All that matters is whether or not the completed design provoked some response. The maximum possible score for the first part of this assessment is 10 points. Jot it down on a separate sheet of paper under the heading – *Personality Factor One*.

You are now ready to complete this assessment by asking your child to draw a picture of a house on a sheet of white, unlined, A4 size paper. The type of building drawn is irrelevant – your child can choose a cottage or a castle, a stately home or a suburban semi. The significant feature of this picture is not the dwelling itself but the child's use of space. Put this drawing aside for the moment, as we will explain how it should be scored in the next chapter.

ILLUSTRATION 1

ILLUSTRATION 2

ILLUSTRATION 3

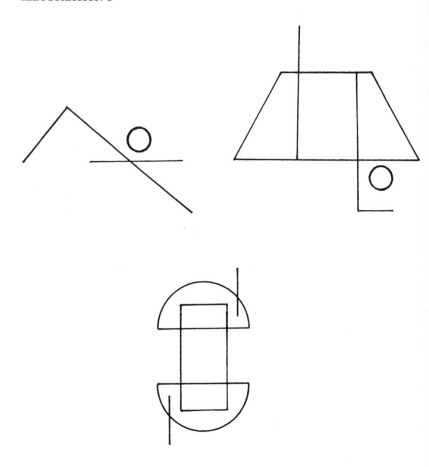

Factor two

This is a timed test, so you will need to watch with either a second hand or digital read-out. Take the time very unobtrusively as many children, eager to give a favourable impression, will work much faster if they realize the drawings are being done against the clock. When this happens the result will not be reliable. Ask your child to copy out the three pictures shown in illustration 3 on to a separate sheet of paper.

Pointing to the designs say something along these lines:

'I would like you to draw these shapes for me. Start here (point to the design on the left), then do this one (indicate the design on the right) and finish here (point to the last one). You mustn't start a new drawing until you have finished the previous one but I don't want you to waste any time. Try and draw each shape as quickly as you can.'

Note the time from the moment the child starts work on the first drawing to the point where the last has been completed. Add up the total time taken – in seconds – to finish all three. Now go straight on to the second part of this assessment, but asking your child to copy the design in illustration 4a, and this time to draw it upside down.

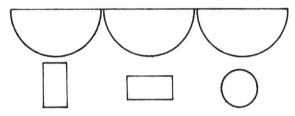

ILLUSTRATION 4a

To make certain that this instruction is quite clear, you may find it helpful to provide a practice session using the design shown below (illustration 4b).

There is no need to time the practice drawing. Point out any mistakes and then, when you feel certain your child knows exactly what is required, start the test itself by having the child draw the second design upside down. Time the attempt and then add this to the total for the first three drawings and make a note of the result under the heading – *Personality Factor Two.*

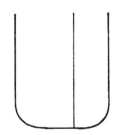

ILLUSTRATION 4b

Factor three

To assess this factor examine four of your child's most recently completed pictures. They must be fully finished pieces of work, not doodles or hasty sketches. You are looking for three possible features: shading, the use of white space and the use of an S-shape.

ILLUSTRATION 5a

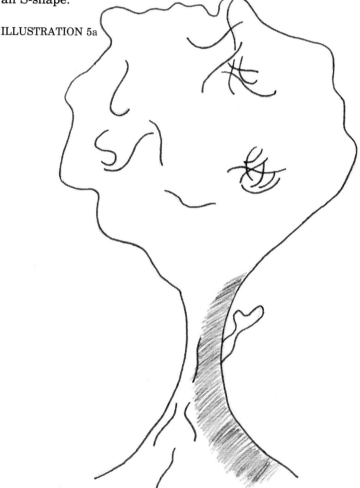

If your child has used less shading than in 5a, award no points. If there is about as much shading as shown here, but less than in 5b, award 2 points.

Shading

Around the age of six or seven, children start using shading as a means of adding depth to their illustrations, and by the age of nine or ten this is usually an established technique. To assess the extent of shading which your child has used, compare each of the pictures with the examples in illustrations 5a–5b.

ILLUSTRATION 5b

If your child's picture contains the same amount of shading as in this picture, award 4 points.

White space

The second feature to look for is the use of white spaces to represent parts of the image. In the first drawing (illustration 6) the child has shaded the paper to represent sky leaving unshaded areas to represent clouds. In illustration 7 white space is used to create rocks among the grass. If your child makes similar use of white space, award that picture 3 points.

S-shape

The final feature to look for is the use of an S-shape as part of the composition. This shape has been outlined in illustrations 8 and 9. The S-shape has been used as a key element of composition by professional illustrators for centuries and is often taught to art students as part of their formal training. Its spontaneous and untutored use by a young child is, therefore, both interesting and psychologically significant.

ILLUSTRATION 6

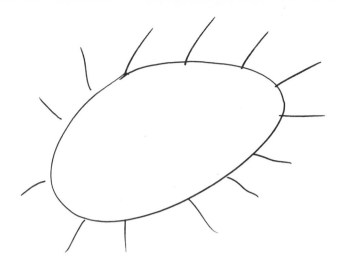

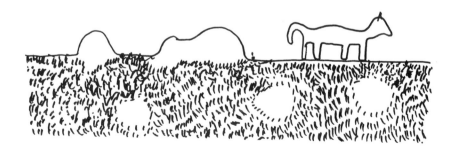

ILLUSTRATION 7

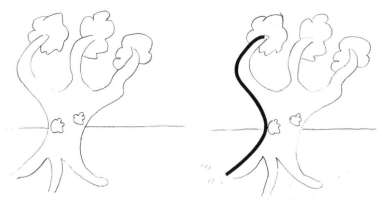

ILLUSTRATION 8   ILLUSTRATION 9

Unlike the other features we have described, the S-shape is often quite tricky to spot and you should study a number of your child's pictures carefully before deciding whether or not it is present. For practice we have provided a second drawing (illustration 10) containing a concealed S-shape. Study the image carefully and see if you can identify the feature before checking your answer at the end of this chapter. Award a further 3 points each time the shape is used in any of your child's sample drawings.

You can now add the score for each picture. The maximum score for each picture is 10 points, making a possible total of 40 points for all four pictures. Enter this score on your record sheet under the heading – *Personality Factor Three*.

Factor four

To assess this factor you simply ask the child to draw a picture of a tree, but your instructions must be explicit: you want the drawing to show a tree, in leaf, standing by itself. The picture should be as complete as the child can make it, with no important details left out.

When the drawing is finished, notice how your child has drawn the shape of the leaves. The most usual way is to represent

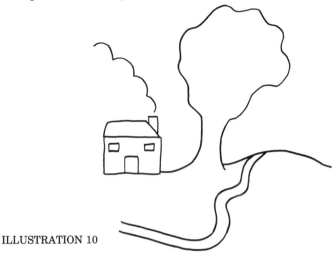

ILLUSTRATION 10

them as a series of curves, as in illustration 11a overleaf. Some children, however, will draw leaves using short lines and sharp angles to produce a jagged edge effect. These features occur to different degrees in the remaining drawings 11b–d. To score your child's picture, compare it with those in the chart and select the best match. Write down your child's score under the heading – *Personality Factor Four.*

Personality factor five

Look through ten recent outdoor scenes your child has drawn or painted. You can include interiors provided these include a large area of the outdoors, as viewed through large windows, the frame of an arch or open doors, for instance. The scene itself is unimportant, and chosen pictures may show towns or cities, landscapes, seascapes or mountain scenes. Now count the number of pictures which include the sun. This can be pictured in full, or partly concealed behind clouds (see illustrations 12a–c).

If your child does not usually do much drawing or painting and you are unable to find ten such pictures, ask him or her to produce them over a period of a few weeks. In this case you should not, of course, give any specific instructions about including the sun. The test is only valid when this is put in or

ILLUSTRATION 11a
Score = 0 points.

ILLUSTRATION 11b
Score = 2 points.

ILLUSTRATION 11c
Score = 4 points.

ILLUSTRATION 11d
Score = 6 points.

ILLUSTRATION 12a

ILLUSTRATION 12b

ILLUSTRATION 12c

left out according to the creative impulse of the child. Score
this factor using the chart below.

Child's age	Number of times sun appears	Score
5–8 years	0– 2	1
	3– 5	2
	6– 8	3
	9–10	4
9 +	0– 2	1
	2– 4	2
	5– 7	3
	8–10	4

Note the final score under the heading – *Personality Factor
Five*

You now possess sufficient information to gain a deep and
accurate insight into the five major personality factors, each of
which are described in detail in Chapter 4.

Solution to missing S-shape

CHAPTER FOUR

What your child's assessment reveals

When reading through the descriptions of the five personality factors assessed in the last chapter, bear in mind that each has both positive and negative features, strengths as well as weaknesses.

Factor one

Extraversion-Introversion
This aspect of personality determines the extent to which children seek out and enjoy other people's company. You have only one score on this factor so far. The assessment is completed by studying your child's picture of the house. As we explained in the last chapter, what matters here is the child's use of space. Some children draw small houses surrounded by large areas of unused paper (see illustration 1). Others design a large house taking up most of the available paper as in illustration 2.

Score your child's effort by comparing it with the pictures on the chart on page 49 (illustrations 3a–e) and selecting the illustration which most nearly matches it in the use of space. Add the scores from both parts of the assessment to produce the final result for the factor of Extraversion-Introversion. Now use the table overleaf to discover what this tells you about your child's rating on this factor.

ILLUSTRATION 1

ILLUSTRATION 2

ILLUSTRATION 3

(a) Score = 2 points

(b) Score = 4 points

(c) Score = 6 points

(d) Score = 8 points

(e) Score = 10 points

Score	Rating
0– 4	More introverted than 85 per cent of other children.
5– 7	More introverted than 65 per cent of other children.
8–12	Both introvert and extravert aspects to the personality, a combination found in most people.
13–15	More extravert than 65 per cent of other children.
16 +	Child is more extravert than 85 per cent of other children.

The terms *extravert* and *introvert* were first used more than fifty years ago by the Swiss psychoanalyst Carl Jung. Since then they have become part of the everyday language, often being employed somewhat critically to describe a person's characteristic approach to life. Told that a child is 'very extravert' or 'highly introverted', many people might expect to find a noisy, boisterous, and rather insensitive youngster in the first case and a pasty-faced little swot, probably friendless and lacking in warmth or humour, on the other.

Needless to say, neither stereotype is accurate, although – as with most caricatures – they contain a grain of truth. In practice, it is fairly rare to meet anybody at the extremes of this factor, since most people possess both introvert and extravert aspects to their personality and should more accurately be termed *midiverts*. This means that the individual can switch from reasonably extravert behaviour – such as enjoying themselves at a lively party – to moderately introvert activities, for example, working or playing on their own for limited periods without any distress. Many psychologists take the view that these variations in personality are caused by inborn differences in the structure of the nervous system.

Some people require a constantly high level of stimulation in order to feel good and work efficiently. Others are at their best in quieter surroundings and find it very hard to tolerate a great deal of bustle, noise and excitement. These differing needs will clearly influence the type of activities each finds enjoyable, the kind of situations they can deal with most effectively and the goals they regard as being of greatest importance in life. The introvert child, for instance, prefers to play with just a few close friends, is better at dealing with objects than people, and performs best on solitary tasks or as one of a small, friendly team. The extravert child by comparison will prefer to have many friends, copes best with social situations and enjoys taking part in group activities.

What to expect from an introvert child

The lower your child's score on this factor the more introverted he or she is likely to prove and the more closely the descriptions given below will apply.

Strengths

Although they generally make fewer friends than extravert children, those friendships are usually deep and lasting. Introverts are self-sufficient and, trusting in their own judgements, less easily swayed by the opinions or prejudices of others. They are able to plan ahead and set themselves realistic goals which they work towards methodically and painstakingly. Because their powers of concentration are high, learning often comes easily to them, so they can master new subjects more efficiently than more extravert children of the same age.

Being cautious introverts plan ahead and weigh the consequences of any action before proceeding, so avoiding the pitfalls awaiting less careful youngsters. Introverted children are prepared to sacrifice short-term rewards for longer-term gains, and so remain motivated while working towards distant goals – for instance, exam passes. They often do best in subjects such as science and technology which demand a methodical and logical approach.

Weaknesses

Introverted youngsters are sometimes less popular with their companions than extravert youngsters, a fact more likely to concern parents than the children themselves. They can be very stubborn, especially when appealed to on emotional rather than logical grounds and, while their tendency not to be easily influenced by the views and opinions of others is admirable in many ways, it may well bring them into conflict with parents and teachers.

Introverts are inclined to adopt an overly pessimistic view of life and tend to suffer from a lack of self-confidence. As a result such children may exaggerate their difficulties, over-estimate their problems and worry far more than is necessary. You may not always realize just how anxious, worried or depressed the introvert child is, however, since they tend to conceal their feelings and find it hard to talk openly about their fears. Because they would rather listen than join in classroom discussions, some teachers may underestimate their true ability and rate them less highly than extravert students who are both more vocal and more socially skilled.

Helping the introverted child

It is essential to recognize and to respect the rights of even a small child to develop into a unique individual rather than grow into a reflection of parental attitudes and ambitions. Do not try to force an introverted child to become more extravert in their preferences and behaviour. You will ultimately fail and, in the process, damage both your relationship and their emotional development. Do not regard his or her outlook as somehow less worthwhile or valid even if it differs remarkably from your own views on life.

Try not to worry if your child seems rather isolated and appears to have fewer friends than other children of the same age. As we have explained, those friendships which are formed will be deep, lasting and extremely rewarding.

Because introverted children are more prone to worrying and less willing to talk over their difficulties than the average child, you will need to provide a great deal of sympathy, understanding and support should problems arise. Do not make the mistake of assuming that, because the child seems very self-sufficient, he or she has no need of your encouragement and guidance. Despite occasional appearances to the contrary, quite the opposite is likely to be true. Remember that introverted children are frequently overly self-critical, pessimistic and lacking in confidence. These aspects of their personality can allow considerable tension to build up unnoticed, even by caring parents, until it reveals itself in some dramatic manner, for instance by truancy or school refusal, withdrawal, temper tantrums or psychosomatic illness.

As with all problems, early detection and prevention is far better – and a great deal easier – than cure. The sooner difficulties are identified and dealt with the easier and most effective treatment will prove.

What to expect from the midivert child

Strengths

As this term implies, the personality of the midivert child lies midway between extraversion and introversion. Such youngsters possess the chameleon-like ability to adapt their behaviour to satisfy the demands of a wide variety of activities and situations. They are quite capable of being sociable and of enjoying the company of others, yet can be just as happy playing alone.

In some ways the midivert child possesses a very helpful balance between the two extremes, being able to appreciate both extravert and introvert activities without ever showing the extremes of behaviour associated with either personality factor. They can talk about themselves and their problems reasonably easily, although there will usually be some part of their lives, certain aspects of their innermost selves, which remain carefully screened from scrutiny.

Midivert children are self-confident and self-sufficient in most situations, but when life gets especially tough, they are prepared to seek help from parents, teachers or friends with a readiness seldom encountered in the more introverted child.

Weaknesses

Although capable of showing both introvert and extravert behaviour, midivert children may never feel completely at ease in either role. They are able to appreciate the positive and negative aspects of each and, as a result, they may never feel completely satisfied with any situation. If in company they yearn to be alone, while if solitary they desire the companionship of other children. Furthermore, if faced with the need to be very sociable or to put up with long periods on their own, midivert children are unable to cope happily or long with the resulting pressures. They become increasingly unhappy, uncertain and unwilling to tolerate the situation.

A midivert child may play happily with a small number of friendly companions but become increasingly anxious if the games become too boisterous or too many others start joining in. At some point he or she will simply refuse to go on playing and withdraw to the sidelines. Equally, while the midivert child can play or work alone for a certain amount of time without feeling too lonely, long periods of isolation will prove unsettling. Because of this somewhat ambivalent attitude midivert children may never enjoy the popularity of the extravert child or take the same enjoyment from solitary pursuits as the introvert.

Helping the midivert child

The key to understanding a child with this type of personality is to appreciate their need for balance and the avoidance of extremes of behaviour. The child should not be obliged to work or play alone either too often or for lengthy periods at a time. Neither should he or she be expected to find much enjoyment in activities which require them to mix with a great many people or be the focus of attention.

How adults respond to midivert children depends, to a great extent, on their own personality. Introverted parents, for example, may regard the child's need for company and desire to take part in stimulating activities as being somehow 'out of character', while extravert parents are likely to be concerned about or puzzled by their child's occasional desire for solitude.

Each makes the mistake of focusing on those aspects of personality which most closely match their own and assuming these to be the key to the child's true character. As we explained when discussing the needs of the introverted youngster, it is essential to respect the child's individuality and to avoid value judgements about their outlook on life. Because midivert children are able to talk about their fears and problems more openly than introverted youngsters, it is easy to fall into the trap of assuming that you can get to the heart of any emotional upset during a friendly chat. Remember that midiverts are perfectly capable of concealing their innermost feelings even when speaking with apparent frankness.

What to expect from the extravert child

Strengths
Their social skills mean that extravert children often have a great many friends their own age and are usually well liked by adults, especially equally extraverted ones. They are less critical – either of themselves or others – than introverted children and approach life with the optimistic confidence of Voltaire's Dr Pangloss who believed that 'all is for the best in this best of all possible worlds'.

Since a way with words is so essential to social success, extravert children usually use language very effectively, discussing ideas, opinions and feelings with considerable fluency. They are prepared to reveal their innermost thoughts more freely than either midivert or introvert children and enjoy being the centre of attention. Given all these attributes it is hardly surprising that they often do well at interviews and show an early interest in advertising, public relations, journalism or broadcasting careers, where these skills can be put to good use.

Weaknesses
As we have already mentioned, the ease with which extravert children make friends has a less positive aspect in that those friendships may be fairly superficial. Such children tend to be impulsive, lacking in caution and unwilling to make short-term sacrifices in order to obtain longer-term rewards.

Extraverts may be less emotionally stable than more introverted children and show rapid mood swings from elation to despondency. They tend to be fairly uncritical when evaluating themselves and their work, an attitude which can result in careless errors and thoughtless conduct. Because they become anxious if isolated, either physically or because of their opinions, such children tend to be more than usually conformist. If mixing with children who are socially skilled and positive in their outlook, this need to belong can prove beneficial. If they get involved with a number of children who hold negative attitudes towards behaviour or school work, however, they will find it hard to resist the pressures to conform.

Helping the extravert child

Parents, especially if rather introverted themselves, may find extravert children hard to understand and even more difficult to handle. Their child's apparently unending desire for stimulation, whether in the form of boisterous and sometimes physically hazardous games, loud music, or lots of equally active companions is usually sufficient to fray the nerves and stretch the patience of even the most understanding adult.

Parents sometimes punish extravert conduct and may, if discipline is enforced strictly, be able to modify their child's behaviour in the short term. But this appearance of conformity masks unchanged, and indeed unchangeable, underlying factors in the child's personality. As he or she grows older and increasingly independent, these characteristics are almost certain to reassert themselves, perhaps even more strongly than might have been the case had they not been repressed in early childhood. The result will be a further alienation and increasing conflict within the family.

As we have stressed in the sections on introverted and midivert children, it is essential to accept your child's right to his or her personal views about life even when these conflict with your own outlook. Rather than attempting to bring about changes – an ultimately fruitless exercise – try to help extraverts channel their abundant enthusiasm and energy into constructive enterprises.

Extravert children sometimes find it hard to work consistently towards long-term goals, and may encounter difficulties in school. Instead of pausing for thought and allowing their brain the chance to come up with a considered answer, they tend to blurt out – or scribble down – the first response which comes into their head. This causes a great many mistakes and can lead teachers to underestimate the child's intellectual abilities. Once again, instead of punishing or blaming children for their behaviour, help them to slow down their responses slightly so that they can check their answers. Ways in which this can be done are explained in Chapter 9. Build on the special skills of extravert youngsters – their confidence, energy, optimism and, especially, their ability to get along well with others.

Personality factor two

Energy focus

Each child can be thought of as having certain reserves of energy which may be focused on everyday activities and challenges. Studies by Professor Raymond Cattell, at the University of Hawaii, have shown that a child's personal 'energy bank' not only determines how he or she behaves but also influences his or her powers of concentration, memory, perseverance and emotional stability.

How to score the assessment

Drawing tests like those you gave to your child provide an accurate assessment of 'energy focus' in youngsters aged five years and older. This is because the concentration needed to carry out the task slows down children with low energy reserves. Those who possess abundant stores of energy, by comparison, produce the drawings more rapidly than most. To identify your child's rating on this factor, compare the time taken – in seconds – to complete both sets of drawings with the table below.

These figures, based on our research, also allow you to compare your child's times with the average scores for children of different ages.

Age	*Energy focus*				
	Low	*Fairly low*	*Average*	*Fairly high*	*High*
5	85+	84–75	74–68	67–72	61 less
6– 7	75+	74–65	64–58	57–52	51 less
8– 9	65+	64–55	54–46	45–40	39 less
10–11	57+	56–48	47–40	39–34	33 less
12+	50+	49–42	41–35	34–30	29 less

Low = only 15 per cent of children have lower energy focus
Fairly low = 30 per cent of children have lower energy focus

Average = 50 per cent of children have lower energy focus
Fairly high = 30 per cent of children have higher energy focus
High = only 15 per cent of children have higher energy focus

For example:
A 6-year-old completing both sets of drawings in 62 seconds, would have an average energy focus.

A child aged 10 who took more than 57 seconds over the tests would have a low energy focus.

An 8-year-old with a total time of 34 seconds has a high energy focus.

As with the extraversion-introversion aspect of personality, the higher or lower your child's score the more closely their responses are likely to correspond with those described below. Children with an average focus of energy will show some of the behaviours associated with both high and low energy focus youngsters.

What to expect from high energy focus children

Such children are willing to invest a tremendous amount of effort and energy in all they do. They search enthusiastically for fresh challenges and have ample reserves of mental and physical strength to bring to bear on life's problems. This gives them above average feelings of confidence and security, together with a considerable capacity for handling stress and coping with emotional upsets.

They usually worry less than low energy focus children and may appear outwardly more serene. They adopt a flexible approach to life and can adapt to new situations or ways of doing things with little or no loss of performance. Changes of school, transfer to a new class, or moving to a different neighbourhood, for example, are unlikely to upset them. In most cases their ability to read, remember and concentrate is above average.

Independent in their outlook and attitudes, high energy focus children tend to pay less attention to advice and instructions from parents and teachers than children with a lower level of energy focus. While this may sometimes irritate or anger adults, it should be remembered that at more advanced levels of study, academic success depends on being able to think independently and to trust one's own judgments. Professor Cattell, for example, has found that this type of child tends to excel at subjects demanding a logical approach and is often attracted by science and technical subjects. The same research revealed that high energy children generally have above average co-ordination, and this skill – combined with their active natures – often helps them do well at most sports.

What to expect from low energy focus children

Because children with low reserves of energy are more prone to psychological stress than most, they need special understanding from parents, who should do their best to cushion them against any emotional upsets. Such children do not, necessarily, experience greater anxiety than the average child, but they tend to respond to such anxiety in ways which are inappropriate and ineffective. In particular, they frequently over-react to stress and lose their temper when upset or fearful.

Low energy focus children tend to be somewhat insecure and are more likely to be influenced by their companions than children with a higher focus of energy, and will wish to conform to group expectations. This can prove helpful to them provided the consensus views are positive, but may lead them into trouble if they get into bad company.

Although there is no overall difference between children with varying degrees of energy focus in terms of either intelligence or school performance, those with low levels tend to have greater difficulty in concentrating for long periods. Being rather lacking in persistence, and too readily distracted, they may react to setbacks in class by simply giving up all attempts to understand the subject.

They may adopt a rather inflexible approach when confronted by unfamiliar or novel tasks and will stick doggedly to this approach even when it becomes glaringly obvious that a different tactic is needed. Unfortunately, this reluctance to rethink their methods of working does not apply if a previously successful procedure leads to unexpected failure. Instead of persisting, they may abruptly abandon it in favour of a far less effective approach. They are not very good at solving mental problems and dislike those demanding a strictly logical approach – such as questions in maths or science, their interests and abilities lying more with artistic subjects. Differences between the kinds of thinking required for success in these different areas of work are described in Chapter 10.

Clearly, the special needs of the low energy focus child call for sympathy and understanding on the part of adults, who should make a special effort to protect them from the inevitable emotional traumas of childhood and guide them towards those areas of study where they are likely to be happiest and most successful. Because they are more dependent on parental guidance and help than the average child, they usually respond well to such efforts and are prepared to accept advice and direction to an extent you would not find with the high energy focus child. Their ambitions need to be looked at carefully and objectively since these children tend to reveal a marked difference between aspirations and actual attainment, often setting themselves goals which are idealistic and unobtainable.

Personality factor three

Sensitivity
Although sensitivity may sound like a rather vague and general term to use in relation to personality, it is used here in a precise way to describe your child's ability to discriminate among events in the world around him and among the ideas and memories in his head. After studying hundreds of children's pictures, administering psychological tests, conducting interviews and examining detailed case histories, Dr Trude Waehmer and her team of researchers at New York University found that children reveal clearly the extent of their sensitivity when drawing and painting.

The characteristic features of pictures created by sensitive children are *shading, white spaces* and *S-shapes*. We have drawn on Dr Waehmer's studies, as well as our own research findings, to produce a scoring system which provides an accurate guide to varying levels of sensitivity, so allowing you to compare your own child's results with those obtained by children in the same age range.

Age of child	Sensitivity		
	Average	Fairly High	High
5	0– 2	4–10	10+
6– 7	0– 4	6–12	12+
8– 9	0– 6	8–14	14+
10–11	0– 8	10–16	16+
12+	0–10	12–20	20+

The higher your child's score on this Personality Factor the more likely it is that he or she will display the abilities and attitudes we describe.

What to expect from the highly sensitive child

Children who score high on sensitivity are also likely to be more than usually intelligent and creative. Although a high level of sensitivity is in many ways useful and desirable, it can be something of a mixed blessing in the younger child. Because such children can detect fine and subtle changes in their surroundings they are far more aware than most youngsters of anything even slightly out of the ordinary. A momentary change of expression, a slight alteration in voice tone or emphasis can alert them to the fact that something unusual may be happening. For instance, parents attempting to conceal marriage difficulties through displays of affection whenever the children are around will not deceive the very sensitive child for long. All forms of pretence and deception, all attempts to mislead or misdirect such youngsters are more likely to fail than to succeed.

Their ability to detect ambiguous responses, slight shifts of mood, minor adjustments to expressions, posture, gesture or gaze makes such children watchful and, perhaps, anxious. At this point neither play-acting nor reassurances will be sufficient to defuse their distress. Indeed, an insistence that 'everything is all right' and there is 'nothing to worry about', may simply increase their uncertainty and concern.

Sensitive children daydream a good deal, have a powerful fantasy life and are easily offended. While their superior intuition often delights adults, their tendency to retreat into a private world of the imagination at the first sign of parental disapproval or in the face of some slight, whether intended or unintended, real or imaginary, usually arouses irritation rather than approval.

Parents, often unaware of the extent of their child's sensitivity, may be mystified by the mercurial behaviour which accompanies it. This is especially likely with two groups of children: the older child, whose high sensitivity may be masked by other, seemingly insensitive reactions, such as displays of indifference, apathy, or aggression; and the very young child whose sensitivity has not yet developed to the point where it is clearly revealed by everyday behaviour. In both cases picture assessments provide a powerful method for gaining essential knowledge of this important personality factor. If the assessment revealed your own child to have average, or above average sensitivity, the following suggestions should enable you to help and guide them most effectively:

Always try to be completely open and entirely honest in your dealings with the child.

Never attempt to cover up or conceal your true feelings about some distressing situation or event. Remember that the sensitive child, well aware that you are upset and unhappy, will become more – not less – anxious if his or her realistic perceptions are persistently denied or casually dismissed.

Because highly sensitive children are usually of above average intelligence, avoid talking down to them, or attempting to fob them off with half-truths. In the long term, anything less than frankness and sincerity is likely to cost you their trust and respect. This does not mean, of course, that you should try to explain the precise reasons for your feelings to children too young to understand the sort of things which make adults anxious or unhappy. It is quite sufficient merely to acknowledge that you are feeling sad or angry, depressed or tired.

Help nurture their creativity. Do not try to separate them from the vivid world of their imagination, because this is important for successful intellectual development. Sensitive children sometimes invent a *fantasy friend* so real to them that they can play happily for hours. Do not worry if this happens with your own highly sensitive child. In time this invisible friend will quietly disappear and real life relationships become increasingly important.

Remember that your child is sensitive to slights and easily takes offence. While we are not suggesting that you should never offer justified and constructive criticisms, avoid sarcastic or disparaging remarks which can cause the highly sensitive child far greater distress than intended. When it becomes necessary to point out mistakes or scold bad behaviour, pick your words carefully and avoid attacking the child in general terms, by calling them 'stupid', 'lazy', 'dirty', or 'bad', for instance. While a less sensitive child will probably not take such words at face value, high scorers have their sense of competence and self-worth seriously undermined by such remarks.

One of the authors, David Lewis, has called this type of abusive comment GIGO statements, a term taken from the world of computing. It stands for Garbage In-Garbage Out, and means simply that if you put rubbish into the computer, rubbish is all you can reasonably expect to get out of it! Where children are concerned, GIGO statements include all those remarks calculated to hurt rather than help. While nobody would deny parents and teachers the right to guide and correct children's behaviour, this can be achieved far more rapidly and successfully through the use of constructive comments. Instead of attempting to humiliate or belittle the youngster, point out faults in a neutral way and offer practical advice about how to act in future.

You can easily identify GIGO statements by asking yourself a simple question: is my comment intended to offer constructive guidance or simply provide a release for my anger, distaste or distress? By all means express such emotions openly to the child – you have every right to your feelings and every right to let your child realize the response his behaviour has provoked. But, at the same time, avoid allowing your anger to express itself in ways which attack and wound emotionally. All children are harmed to some extent by the repeated use of GIGO comments, but our research has shown that the highly sensitive child is far more vulnerable to such verbal assaults.

Personality factor four

Aggression
Dr Trude Waehmer's studies, which have proved useful in assessing a child's level of sensitivity through their pictures, have also provided a means of identifying the personality factor of aggression. She has found that the use of sharp angles and jagged lines in parts of the picture where one might expect to see smooth curves is closely related to aggressive traits. This was explored in the assessment by asking the child to draw leaves on a tree. Children low on this factor will represent them using a series of curves, while more aggressive children are likely to use straight lines and acute angles.

Score	Amount of aggression suggested
0	None
2	Low
4	Medium
6	High

One theory as to why angles are such a good guide to aggression suggests that the child is unconsciously creating shapes associated with violence and destruction. Sharp angles occur in objects used to attack and injure others, such as knives, swords, axes, scissors, daggers and spears. It has been argued that these feature prominently in the aggressive youngster's fantasy world and so find ready expression in drawings which otherwise contain no aggressive features.

It may be that children who use angles and straight lines in their pictures also show far more obvious signs of aggression – bullying, fighting, being cruel to children or animals, throwing temper tantrums, acting destructively and so on. It is also possible, however, that children who score high on this factor only reveal their aggression in specific situations – at home but not at school, for example – or confine aggression to a fantasy world. Such children may also behave in ways which, while not openly hostile, angry or destructive represent a form of passive aggression. Persistent stubbornness and a consistent refusal to do what is wanted or expected of them are techniques adopted by the aggressive child for expressing an inner anger.

Helping the aggressive child

When caused by a threatening situation aggression takes the form of a shortlived mood experienced by a child not normally hostile or angry. As a Personality Factor, aggression reflects a tendency to respond with hostility – either actively or passively – in situations which other children would deal with non-aggressively. Such aggression is often associated with a low tolerance of frustrations and an absence of the vital skills necessary for coping with setbacks in a more effective manner.

A frequent response of adults to aggression is to become equally hostile and, frequently, physically violent themselves. Bullies, for example, are often shown the 'errors of their ways' by being spanked or caned. While this may satisfy the outrage of parents or teachers, it is unlikely to reduce aggressive behaviour. The chief lesson learned by children who have been assaulted by somebody taller and stronger than they are is that violence is a perfectly acceptable means of persuasion – so long as you have might, if not right, on your side. However annoying, frustrating or frightening the aggressive child's behaviour may be, therefore, the least effective method for handling it is by means of an equally aggressive response.

If your child's drawings and/or behaviour reveal aggression, we suggest that you start by looking back through earlier pictures to discover whether the use of angles in place of curves has been a persistent feature. If it has developed over a period of weeks or months, try to recall any major changes in his or her life which might have happened around the time these features began appearing. Possible events include the birth of a new baby; conflicts in your own marriage; the move to a new school or a different neighbourhood; the loss of a close friend; falling behind in class because of absence through illness; the death of a friend or relative; the transfer to a higher class; having a new form teacher and the physical changes occurring at puberty.

If your child's drawings do not provide clues, you should still try to discover the reasons behind aggressive behaviour instead of simply attempting to reduce that aggression through disapproval and punishment. Aggression is often the last resort of a youngster who cannot see any other way of expressing his or her feelings, or of changing a situation which is regarded as intolerable.

Long-term reduction of aggression can only be brought about by providing the child with new and more acceptable ways of displaying emotions and controlling events. Where the aggression is expressed in terms of a refusal to conform to family rules or comply with reasonable requests, ask yourself whether the child may not be copying these responses from other members of the family, especially adults or older children. Busy parents can unintentionally provide a model for such conduct by refusing perfectly reasonable requests from the child:

'Not now ...' snaps the father when asked for help with homework.

'Can't you see I'm too busy to pay attention to you now,' protests the harassed mother.

When this is a frequent response the child may come to adopt the same tactic and say 'no' more often than 'yes' when dealing with adults.

However busy your work schedule, try to set aside some specific period during the day to be with your child to talk to him or her and help. Make it clear, and to other members of the family as well, that this is a special time when he or she can expect your undivided attention. You should also make it clear that requests at other times during the day may not be dealt with immediately. Children are usually very happy with this kind of approach, provided you keep your word and give your undivided attention at the specified time.

Finally, consider how much aggression – verbal or otherwise – you show towards the child. Many adults boss children around in ways which they would never tolerate from another adult. When parental attitudes are typified by curtness and rudeness, it is hardly surprising the child adopts similar tactics, either when dealing with adults or with other youngsters. The open expression of aggression by children who score high on this personality factor is often an accurate reflection of levels of aggression within the home. Aggression as an emotional response to situations which the child finds intolerable or threatening is discussed more fully in Chapter 5.

Personality factor five

Dependence

This personality factor influences the extent to which children rely on their own judgments when making important decisions or trying to solve problems. We assess this by looking at the frequency with which children include the sun in their pictures. The link between this feature of drawings and paintings and dependency was first identified by Dr Jan Loney, of the University of Iowa. His research showed clearly that the more often the sun is included the greater that child's reliance on advice and guidance from adults. The chart below shows the degree of dependency revealed by the scores obtained from this assessment.

Score	Degree of dependency shown by contrast with others of the same age
1	Far more independent
2	Slightly more independent
3	About as dependent
4	Much more dependent

What to expect from the independent child

As one would expect, independent children think for themselves and are less likely to be influenced by the opinions of others than the less self-reliant youngster.

Helping the independent child

In many ways, this is a very desirable state of affairs, since children should always be encouraged to develop their own ideas about life and to learn from firsthand experience. The independent child needs far less encouragement than most to explore and find out about the world. Indeed, many parents of highly independent children tell us that the main problem is containing and controlling the powerful desire to think and act for themselves.

This leads us to the major difficulty presented by these independent attitudes, the child's considerable reluctance to follow parental advice, or to accept adult guidance. When very young it is of course essential to protect independent children from making serious mistakes and to ensure that their curiosity does not lead them into danger. As the child grows in strength and maturity, however, it is very important to relax parental controls as much as possible so as to place only few restrictions on their desire for independence. Avoid being overprotective and do not worry too much if the child gets into scrapes now and again. They tend to be far more resilient than the dependent child and will not easily be discouraged or deterred from their desire to find out at first hand.

Keep family rules and restrictions to a minimum, but ensure that those you do impose are applied firmly and consistently, since it is only in this way that the independent child can acquire a sense of self-discipline. Do not feel too concerned if school reports mention a lack of discipline. Experience has shown that very independent children do not conform easily to classroom rules and their tendency to question rather than accept what they are told at face value will greatly irritate less tolerant teachers.

Instead of attempting to spoon-feed the child with information or advice, act more as a resource centre making available as many stimulating and interesting ideas as possible. Having set the child in the right direction, step back and allow him or her to take responsibility for what follows.

What to expect from the dependent child

Dependency in children is usually revealed in a reluctance to take responsibility for their own ideas or actions and a desire to seek help from adults, or older children, even when working on tasks well within their capabilities. In class the dependent child may get into the habit of copying from his or her neighbour and constantly looking for help, advice and reassurance from teachers.

Helping the dependent child

If the sun appears frequently in your child's drawings, but he or she seems fairly independent when at home, it will be useful to check with teachers to discover whether he or she is showing greater dependency in class. Equally, if your child appears rather over-dependent at home, find out whether this behaviour is also found in school.

In children aged seven and older, excessive dependency should be reduced since it is only by developing a self-sufficient and independent attitude towards life's challenges that children achieve successful social and intellectual growth. Do not attempt to bring about these changes all at once, however. Introduce opportunities for greater independence in thought and actions gradually so as to avoid arousing excessive anxiety. When a child has got into the habit of turning to adults for help and guidance, an abrupt refusal to provide such assistance can easily induce emotional stress.

Start rewarding independent behaviour by acknowledging and praising their efforts, however unsuccessful these may be. When the child acts in a dependent way adopt a neutral approach, neither encouraging, nor of course punishing their requests for help.

Allow your child a real say in family decision-making and encourage him or her to organize and carry out projects around the house. Let him or her plan outings, choose the decor for his or her own room and so on. Never disparage the child's ideas, however mistaken you feel them to be. Having asked for suggestions, allow the child to put his or her schemes into practice, even though you can see in advance they are not going to work out.

Dependent children usually fear and try to avoid mistakes because they believe adults will like and admire them less. This anxiety can only be eliminated through the firsthand discovery that your love is not dependent on them always doing everything perfectly.

As you can see, the five personality factors which one can assess easily and accurately from drawings and paintings exert a powerful influence over almost everything your child says or does, thinks or feels, aims for and attains. These factors, as we explained at the start of Chapter 3, are more or less permanent aspects of their character resulting from inborn features of their psychological make-up. No less important in terms of everyday behaviour, however, are the emotions which a child either expresses or keeps bottled up.

Emotions are not always the outer expression of an underlying personality factor. At times they can be the outward and visible signs of an intense internal conflict which can cause them to behave in a way which seems 'out of character'. It is the moment when the usually non-aggressive child lashes out, the time when the normally dependent youngster acts with remarkable independence, the occasion when an extravert child becomes withdrawn and uncommunicative. Such emotions are discussed in detail in Chapter 5, in which we tell you how to use drawings and paintings to unravel the often puzzling actions of the emotional child.

CHAPTER FIVE

How pictures reveal emotions

Martin, a lively six-year-old, likes red better than any other colour in his paintbox. Red cars drive along streets flanked by tall, red, buildings. He enjoys painting fires because they offer such scope for his use of reds, as garish flames leap from blazing buildings to redden the sky with their glow. Martin also manages to splash a lot of red around when painting subjects which could just as well be coloured differently. People in his pictures have red faces and wear red clothes, ships have red hulls and funnels, the walls of rooms are decorated with red stripes.

Mary, aged seven, chooses blue whenever she can and especially enjoys painting ocean scenes or landscapes with vast expanses of blue sky. But, like Martin, she manages to include blue in pictures even where other colours would do just as well. Human figures sport blue shirts and blouses, blue trousers and skirts. They drive blue cars, eat off blue tablecloths, sleep in beds beneath blue quilts and live in houses with bright blue front doors and window frames.

Although it might seem that each child's colour preference is merely a matter of taste, research has shown it to have a deeper significance. When children prefer a particular colour so consistently that it comes to dominate the majority of their pictures, the choice provides us with important insights into their emotions. Even without more obvious signs in their everyday attitudes and behaviour, it becomes possible to identify underlying feelings of frustration or fear, guilt or depression, anxiety or anger. We can tell, for example, whether the child is aggressive and hostile or mature and self-possessed, dependent or self-sufficient, outgoing or self-contained.

In the next two chapters we explore the intimate relationship between colour choice and emotional responses, describing the meaning of a particular preference and explaining how children's pictures enable us to understand their innermost feelings. We will be demonstrating a two-second test for emotional health and showing you how to identify a 'life crisis' which could be causing anxiety or depression.

Colours and emotions

The close link between colours and feelings becomes less surprising when we consider the extent to which colours are used to describe and even create emotions:

We talk of seeing *red* when angry or being *white* with rage.

People are said to be *green* with envy while jealousy is, of course, the *green-eyed* monster.

When things start going badly we may feel so *blue* that we end up *browned off* or in a mood of *black* despair.

We feel in the *pink* when life is good and start viewing the world through *rose-coloured* glasses.

Cowardice is deemed being *yellow*, although we may later concede that our views on the coward's behaviour were *coloured* by emotions.

Even the word 'colour' has come to arouse strong feelings through its association with racial prejudice. Special colour schemes are used in places as diverse as hospitals and hotels, private homes and concerts halls, airports and theatres to create a particular type of mood or arouse a desired emotional response.

Blue and green are relaxing, which is why the designers of aircraft interiors and hospital waiting rooms so often favour them.

Red arouses us

Yellow produces feelings of security

Black conveys an atmosphere of sinister mystery

Purple and gold suggest luxury and wealth

White is associated with purity or clinical efficiency. Doctors and nurses wear white more because of its power to arouse the right kinds of emotion than for any practical reasons.

Research has shown that these moods have a powerful physical as well as a psychological component. When volunteers, wired to instruments which record such stress-related functions as heart rate and blood pressure, are placed in an all-blue room, there is a significant drop in bodily arousal. If they are then moved to a room dominated by red, the recording devices indicate a sharp increase in physical tension, even though the volunteers do not feel an increasing stress. It is only natural, therefore, that child psychologists have long been fascinated by the link between colour preference and emotions.

Extensive studies have shown that colour choice reflects both passing moods and longer-term aspects of emotional health. It is an association which starts in the nursery and continues into adult life. One of the most detailed investigations into the role of colour in children's art has been carried out by Dr Rose Alschuler, former chairperson of the National Commission for Young Children in Washington D.C., who has spent more than a decade studying the pictures of several hundred young painters. She also interviewed them and had each child complete a detailed questionnaire of various aspects of his or her emotions.

We have put Dr Alschuler's findings to the test in our own clinical work and devised a simple technique for analysing the emotions of childhood through the use of coloured images. However, you must bear in mind that the interpretations given below only apply when the colour involved has become such a firm favourite that it dominates more than 50 per cent of a child's pictures. The stronger a child's attachment to a particular colour the more closely the descriptions below will apply.

Red as the dominant colour

When red dominates paintings this usually indicates hostility and aggression. An increasing use of red, until it is established as the dominant colour, frequently occurs during periods of emotional difficulty or after a distressing event. (See illustration 5 in the colour section.)

Red is especially helpful in identifying aggressive feelings in the more introverted child who, as we explained in the last chapter, often finds it difficult to talk about their deepest emotions. When red is being used in response to some particularly traumatic episode, its dominance will almost certainly decline as the child's feelings of aggression diminish. Where red has become firmly established as the colour of choice, however, it is likely that the child is given to outbursts of temper and may well be more emotional than most. In these cases, red is likely to be associated with the other signs of anger in their pictures, such as the use of sharp angles instead of curves described in Chapter 3. In this case aggression may be an aspect of personality rather than the result of a short-lived emotional response. Ways of helping the more consistently aggressive child are described in Chapter 6.

Blue as the dominant colour

The dominant use of blue shows that the child is growing away from the impulsive emotional responses of early childhood towards more stable feelings and behaviour. (See illustration 6 in the colour section.) Blue is a sign of greater reflectivity and suggests an increasing sense of self-confidence and self-sufficiency. At this time the child may well be expressing this greater maturity by taking an increasing interest in social activities, in play-groups or infant school, for example.

The preference for blue shows that the child is acquiring the ability to control his or her emotions and focus feelings on particular events or situations. This more adult approach to life contrasts markedly with the responses of infants who will, typically, express their emotions in a wild outburst. The increased use of blue, combined with a decrease in emotional behaviour, should not mislead you, however, into thinking that the child is entirely happy about conforming to adult expectations about the manner and the extent of expression of emotions.

During the transitional stage from the uninhibited and impulsive conduct typical of infancy to the more controlled approach of the older child, considerable conflict can be experienced. Children may secretly yearn to remain infantile in their responses, although they realize that it is essential to react in a restrained and 'grown up' way if they are to gain the approval of parents and teachers. This desire to revert to earlier, less restricted ways of responding to set-backs and successes remains with most people throughout their life.

Many adults would love to be able to bawl with the uninhibited anguish of a baby when life plays them a mean trick or whoop with uninhibited delight when hard-fought victories are won. Indeed, several forms of therapy make use of a reversion to childlike responses as a means of liberating locked-in emotional impulses. During treatment, patients are encouraged to express their feelings freely, without restraint, in order to escape psychologically harmful inhibitions and tightly controlled emotions.

If your child starts using blue more often than other colours, bear in mind that, despite a more restrained and mature outlook on life, there could still remain some resentment and conflict. Encourage him or her to give vent to these feelings occasionally, either by crying unashamedly or – more agree-ably – by laughing loud and long.

Yellow as the dominant colour

The child who consistently chooses yellow as his or her dominant colour is enthusiastic, outgoing and more emotional than most. (See illustration 7 in the colour section.) Such children are also more likely to be dependent on adults and constantly seek their approval or guidance. These children are often attention-seeking, sometimes showing off by boasting or clowning around in order to attract notice from parents and teachers.

When the preference for yellow is recent – a matter of days or weeks – it tells you that your child is passing through a phase during which there is a strong need to win your support and understanding. If he or she is showing a greater dependen-cy than usual, it is a good idea to look back over their work to identify the moment when this colour started to dominate more than half their pictures. You may then be able to relate the onset of dependency to some specific event that may have undermined feelings of security – the move to a higher form, a different school or a new neighbourhood, for example. When dependency is a more firmly established response, use the procedures described in Chapter 4 to help your child develop greater self-confidence and self-sufficiency.

Green as the dominant colour

Children who prefer green to any other colours are usually more self-reliant and mature than others of the same age. They tend to be somewhat unemotional youngsters who approach life in a fairly restrained and cool – even cold – manner. You are unlikely, for instance, to find them either laughing uproariously or crying uninhibitedly. Despite their self-sufficiency they generally get along well with others and display above-average leadership skills. (See illustration 8 in the colour section.)

Purple or black as the dominant colour

Children who use either purple or black as the main colour in more than half their pictures are sending out a cry for help. (See illustration 9 in the colour section.) The excessive use of these colours is usually associated with unhappiness and deep depression. You will normally only find them used extensively during short periods of emotional distress following some event that has been deeply upsetting. It is essential to find out what is causing their feelings of depression so that you can help put matters right.

Sometimes you will find that a simple misunderstanding has produced the upset, as in the case of a six-year-old boy whose father was going abroad for an extended business trip overseas. The child, having overheard an argument between his parents the night before his father left, came to the conclusion that they had split up for good. This notion was fostered by the fact that his best friend's mother and father had parted only a few weeks earlier. His mood of despair at the prospect of never seeing his father again led to a spate of dismal, black-dominated paintings. Because the boy was rather introverted, he could not express these fears to his mother and his outward behaviour remained calm and controlled. It was only on seeing her son's deeply gloomy paintings that she realized something was wrong and, having found out the cause of his unhappiness, was able to reassure him.

Even when the problems are far more complex and much less readily solved, an early identification of such difficulties usually makes them easier to overcome. If black and purple are dominant over a period of several months, they indicate that the child's depression is no passing mood, but the expression of a generally despondent and pessimistic attitude towards life. Such children will require long-term support and guidance in order to resolve the conflicts and confusions responsible for their pessimistic view of the world.

The meaning of overpainting

A significant feature of some pictures is the child's use of overpainting. Here, after painting with one colour, another is used to cover it up. Part of a blue sky might have been overpainted with red, for example, portions of a green lawn covered with yellow, or a red house painted black.

Overpainting indicates that the emotions being expressed through the use of the first colour are being hidden or covered up with feelings associated with the second. A child who first painted predominantly in red and later overlaid this with black, may be revealing feelings of depression over his earlier anger. Similarly, yellow overpainted by green may express a desire to conceal feelings of happiness.

An understanding of overpainting provides us with a better appreciation of a child's inhibitions and conflicts – why, for example, is the child who overpaints red with black so depressed by his or her angry feelings? Being able to express hostility is no less important to healthy emotional development than the ability to display feelings of love, warmth, and tenderness.

Why does the 'green over yellow' child worry about feeling happy? Could it be that enjoyment is seen as being wrong and so joy has come to arouse anxiety? Such a response is not all that rare among children whose parents take an overly serious view of life and are lacking in a sense of humour.

The meaning of colour mixing

Where areas of a picture have been overpainted repeatedly with several different colours, an absence of emotional restraint and maturity is indicated. Such mixing reveals a lack of sensitivity to colour differences and the haphazard use of materials. Rather than attempting to reproduce some particular image or feeling, the child is simply messing around.

Colour mixing is usually found only in the pictures of very young children. When present in the work of children aged four years or older, it suggests that the child is still emotionally immature and may not be developing concepts of self-control and restraint as rapidly as others. In such cases you should provide greater opportunities for him or her to act in mature and independent ways. Use the procedures described in Chapter 4 for enhancing a child's independence.

So far we have looked at emotional assessment in terms of colour, because this approach provides such an easy guide to a child's feelings. Research has also shown, however, that one can make important assessments of emotions using drawings and sketches entirely without colour. This rapid but reliable drawing test can be used to provide an early indication of any emotional problems ahead.

A two-second test for emotional health

One of the most remarkable findings to emerge from studies into the relationship between drawings and emotions is a simple test that offers a reliable method for assessing a child's psychological health. It requires nothing more complicated than a paper and pencil and can be completed in just a couple of seconds. All you have to do is ask the child to draw a circle and note the direction in which it is drawn.

Despite its simplicity, this test has been found to provide a clear early warning of possible emotional problems. A positive result indicates that the child is probably more vulnerable to such difficulties than most. In the study from which this technique was developed, Professor Theodore Blau, an eminent US psychologist and president of the American Psychological Association, asked more than 100 children, all aged around 9, to draw circles. As they did so, he looked to see whether it was drawn in a clockwise or anti-clockwise direction. He then carefully monitored each child's emotional health over the next fifteen years. The results were remarkable.

Anticlockwise   *Clockwise*

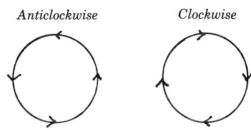

ILLUSTRATION 1

Among the group of children who had drawn their circles in an anticlockwise direction, only 2 per cent ever experienced any major emotional problems. Among the group who had drawn their circles in a clockwise direction, however, this figure rose to 22 per cent. Emotional problems of a less serious nature were also more likely to occur in the remaining 78 per cent of the clockwise group, than in the 98 per cent of the anticlockwise group. So valuable does Professor Blau consider this simple drawing assessment that he now uses it regularly in his psychology practice.

Although the exact mechanisms linking direction of drawing and emotional health have yet to be fully understood, Professor Blau believes that the preferred movement is linked to brain function. As is widely known, the human brain consists of two hemispheres, only partly separated by a deep cleft. In most people the left hemisphere, which controls movement on the right side of the body, is dominant. This hemisphere is concerned with logical reasoning, language and the manipulation of symbols. The right hemisphere, controlling movements on the left side of the body, is less involved with logical operations than with creativity, fantasy and the imagination. Professor Blau suggests that the spontaneous drawing movement represents an unconscious expression of brain dominance.

A child who draws circles in an anticlockwise direction, does so because his left hemisphere is dominant. A clockwise movement, however, may indicate dominance by the right hemisphere, and this could be associated with an imbalance in the brain. It does not matter whether the child is right or lefthanded. The circle test is only valid when applied to children aged six years or older since, below this age, the functioning of the hemisphere has not developed to a point where spontaneous drawing movements have any significance.

The triple circle test

A second, slightly more complex, circle drawing test may be used to make similar predictions with children as young as two or three. Like the first assessment it takes only moments to complete and yet it can produce reliable results. Start by drawing three Xs on a sheet of plain paper, as shown below:

X   X

X

Do not worry if they are not exactly the same size or distance apart as those illustrated, as their purpose is merely to provide the child with three marks around which to draw. Now ask your child to draw a circle around each of the Xs in turn and note the direction (clockwise or anticlockwise) chosen. For the second part of the assessment, ask your child to produce a drawing exactly like that of the snowman in illustration 2. Make certain that the sun is included and, as each circle is produced, observe the direction of movement. If even one of those circles is drawn clockwise, your child is probably slightly more vulnerable to emotional problems than most.

The fact that your child drew every single circle using an anticlockwise movement does not offer any guarantee that he or she will never experience any emotional problems. Nor are we saying that children who produce clockwise circles will

1

2

1 The picture painted by a 10-year-old in February before his problem behaviour began

2 One of John's earliest paintings as he underwent therapy. The dominant themes are hostility, aggression and a sense of isolation

3

4

3 Created in November, the mood of John's painting is one of almost Wagnerian gloom – the sense of unhappiness profound

4 By June, when John painted this picture, the family were happier and far more united. The boy has started to accept his stepfather and is moving closer to his mother

5

6

5 Red as the dominant colour

6 Blue as the dominant colour

7 Yellow as the dominant colour

8 Green as the dominant colour

9 Purple and black as the dominant colours

7

8

9

inevitably experience emotional difficulties. Remember that the majority of children in Professor Blau's study, no matter how they drew their circles, had no serious problems with their emotions during the many years his study lasted.

ILLUSTRATION 2

CHAPTER SIX

How pictures reveal anxiety and depression

When emotional problems arise, anxiety is often a prime cause and depression frequently an end-product. There are, however, two good reasons why the underlying fears can go undetected by even observant and caring adults. For one thing, children can be made anxious by challenges and tasks which their parents could handle with ease. When we are not afraid of something, it is often hard to understand how anybody could possibly find it frightening. Our adult competence makes it difficult for us to view the world through the eyes of a child.

Secondly, while the symptoms of excessive anxiety – crying, white-faced misery, a reluctance to join in with some activities and a refusal even to consider taking part in others – are usually all too obvious, it is much harder to detect lower levels of anxiety. Children can suffer quite considerable distress without showing any clear outward signs – at least in the short term – of their inner turmoil. They may cry a little more than other children, but not excessively so. Their reluctance to do certain things may be put down to obstinacy. Their bouts of mild illness attributed to a lack of physical stamina rather than signs of psychological stress. In other words the anxiety responsible for so much of what they say and do remains undetected until it has built to a point when something dramatic occurs. The risk is, of course, all the greater with introvert and midivert youngsters who, as we pointed out earlier, tend to keep their feelings to themselves. Even at a level which makes detection difficult, anxiety can undermine physical and emotional health, restrict development and impair performance.

We start by describing how you can find out whether your child has an overly anxious approach to life in general or only becomes fearful in particular circumstances. We can then consider depression and how it is likely to arise whenever sufficient anxiety is created to trigger a life crisis. To assess anxiety you require six recent pictures in which your child has drawn or painted the human figure. If none are available, ask for some to be drawn especially for you, without explaining that you intend using them to carry out an assessment. These are best produced over a period of three or four days to prevent the child from getting bored and rushing the last few pictures. Explain that you want full-length portraits of six people – they can be male or female, adult or child. Ask your child to draw them as carefully as possible.

When completed, examine each drawing for the following signs of anxiety:

1 Omissions

2 Distortions

3 Heavy lines

4 Turned-down mouth

5 Raised arms

6 Arms turned inwards

Studies by Dr Leonard Handler, of the University of Tennessee, and Dr Joseph Reyger, of Michigan State University, have shown that every one of these easily identifiable features is associated with above-average levels of anxiety in children aged 5–14 years. Count the number of features present in your child's pictures. The higher the total the greater the underlying anxiety is likely to prove.

Omissions

These may be obvious, the absence of hands or feet, for example, or more subtle, such as missing eyebrows, lips or ears, a failure to draw in the fingers, buttons left off a coat, laces omitted from shoes.

The drawing below was made by Tania, a normally cheerful six-year-old who became withdrawn and moody after going to hospital for a minor operation. At first her parents attributed these changes in their daughter's behaviour to a natural weakness after surgery. When the little girl remained unsettled three months after leaving hospital, however, they sought our advice. Tania's drawings clearly showed that she was very anxious and it seemed likely that these fears were the underlying cause of her withdrawal and moods. The pictures did more than merely express her anxiety, they strongly suggested its cause. A marked feature of Tania's work was

ILLUSTRATION 1

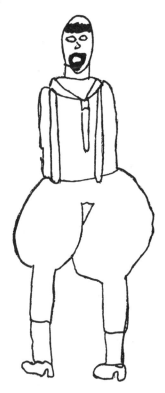

a recurring medical theme. More than half her paintings, and many of her drawings, depicted some kind of hospital activity. She drew ambulances arriving at casualty, she painted wards with white-coated doctors and patients lying bandaged in bed.

When a child dwells on some particular subject you can be fairly certain that the topic is a focus of their emotional concern. Tania's pictures suggested that her anxiety might be due to fears over returning to hospital. Gentle questioning revealed that this was indeed the case. Tania had become convinced that the spell in hospital had been a punishment for bad behaviour and that she would be sent back if she was ever 'naughty' again. By giving the necessary reassurances, Tania's parents were able to set their daughter's mind at rest and she quickly became as cheerful and outgoing as ever.

As you can see in illustration 1, Tania's drawing has three significant omissions. Both arms are missing, she has left out the mouth – although a space has been left for it in the beard – and the eyes have no pupils. Leaving out the arms is especially common in drawings made by anxious children, and often relates to a particular life crisis. The nature of such a crisis, and the way in which it affects the child's pictures, is described later.

Distortions

The rather grotesque image, shown in illustration 2, the work of eight-year-old Billy, was drawn during an unsettled period of the boy's life. His parents had been obliged to move to the city from the country village where he had been born and brought up, after his father, a farm manager, was made redundant.

While searching for a house, the family lived with relatives and the atmosphere quickly became strained. We later discovered that Billy believed they would never have a home of their own again, missed his friends and found life in the big city confusing and rather frightening. His drawings at this time revealed many signs of anxiety, the picture being an excellent example of distortions, which are especially noticeable in the head and right shoulder.

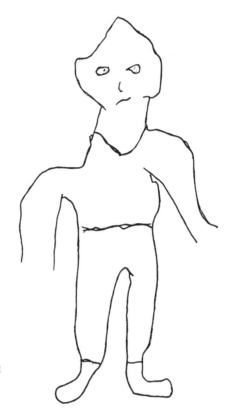

ILLUSTRATION 2

Heavy pressure

When the child applies more pressure to the drawing imple-
ment than is required to create a clear line, it suggests that
inner stresses are revealing themselves through excessive
muscle tension. The greater the pressure the stronger the
anxiety behind it. The quickest and easiest way of discovering
if overly heavy pressure has been used is to apply the touch
test. This only works when the pictures have been drawn on
normal weight paper.

Just run your fingertips along the underside of each drawing
to see whether the pencil or pen point has indented the paper
sufficiently to create a series of easily detectable ridges. If

present, score the drawing as showing unusually heavy pressure.

Turned-down mouth
Upraised arms
Arms turned inwards

In a study of more than 700 drawings, Dr Cynthia Fox and her colleagues at Yale University discovered that all these features are clear signs of underlying anxiety. If they are found together in the picture their warning message becomes even more urgent.

When Colin made the drawing shown in illustration 3, he had just started at a new school. As you can see this contains two of the three signs described. The mouth is turned down and the arms are raised more than 45 degrees above the body. At the time it was drawn, Colin seemed fairly happy although he was a quiet, introverted child not given to any great displays of emotion. His first term's report had been reasonably satisfactory, he had made a few friends of his own age and his behaviour had not changed significantly since moving to the school.

Although neither his parents nor his teachers knew it at the time, however, Colin had become the victim of a vicious protection racket at the school. Organized by much older boys, it exacted a weekly payment from the smaller pupils in return for which they escaped being beaten up. Colin never said anything to his parents, but secretly stole small amounts of money from them to meet his dues. He remained silent even after being caught and punished by his father for stealing. It was only after a chance meeting with the authors that the signs of anxiety in their son's drawings became apparent to them and led to a drastic reassessment of his true feelings.

Once alerted to Colin's difficulties, his mother was able gradually to break through the barriers of fear and natural reserve which had forced him to suffer in silence for so many months. The gang quickly went out of business and the little boy's life was no longer made miserable five days out of seven.

ILLUSTRATION 3

If your child's drawings include a turned-down mouth, arms raised more than 45 degrees above the body, or hands turned inwards – as shown in illustration 3 – then unacceptably high levels of anxiety are being revealed. Even if just one of these signs appears consistently in your child's drawings he or she must be assumed to be more than usually anxious about some, or perhaps many, aspects of life. The greater the number present the higher the level of anxiety being revealed and the more probable it becomes that such fears are undermining self-confidence, happiness and health. As we explained earlier, childhood fears can be caused by many situations, circumstances and activities that appear trivial to adults. They need not be as dramatic or as profound as those described in the brief case histories above in order to generate damagingly high levels of anxiety.

Once you appreciate that a child is experiencing anxiety, you can often uncover and resolve the causes without too much difficulty. Even if nothing can be done to remove the source of their fears, it is still possible to provide support and practical guidance to help them through a difficult period. A frequent source of anxiety are difficulties over making friends and becoming accepted as part of the group. Ways in which these specific problems can be identified and overcome are explained in Chapter 7. Anxiety, often associated with depression, can also be created by an especially upsetting or distressing event. The emotions aroused may then continue long after the moment of trauma has passed. Such an incident is often called a life crisis.

Pictures and life crises

The term 'life crisis' describes any event which is sufficiently disturbing to bring about significant changes in feelings, attitudes or behaviour. Such changes may last any time from just a few days to the rest of one's life. Such a crisis in an adult may be brought about by bereavement, the loss of a job, the break-up of an intimate relationship, the end of a close friendship, children leaving home for good, an obligatory move to a new neighbourhood or serious physical illness.

Some people believe that such a life crisis only happens to

adults, but studies have shown that children too pass through many periods of emotional stress which can reasonably be regarded as marking a crisis point in their life. It is, of course, important for parents to be aware of these times of trauma if they are to provide the help and support essential to see the child through the crisis without lasting harm being done. This is not always as easy to do as one might think, since the changes in behaviour and outlook brought about by the event are sometimes hard to understand and even harder to tolerate. These may include temper tantrums, excessive crying and a readiness to burst into tears, apathy, withdrawal, the destruction of property, sullen silences, bad language and a marked refusal to accept help or respond well to sympathy. Any of these can be so irritating that parents can easily give up and abandon the child to his or her misery. This is especially likely to happen if the cause of the crisis appears 'silly' or 'trivial'.

This is well illustrated by the case of nine-year-old Philip, a good-looking boy who had a birthmark just below his right shoulder. Until he started at a new school he had hardly been aware of this fairly trivial blemish. On the first games afternoon, however, it was brought to his attention by the ridicule of other boys. Philip's obvious distress at these jokes only made his companions all the more eager to mock and tease him. He soon became withdrawn and unhappy. He feigned illness and even played truant rather than having to play games. After a time he began staying away from classes as well to avoid the constant teasing. For a long time he felt too ashamed and embarrassed to tell his parents why, all of a sudden, he had become so unhappy at school. When he finally did blurt out the reason his mother, perhaps relieved that his explanation was so much more 'trivial' than she had feared, dismissed it far too lightly.

'Don't be silly, Phil,' she remembers saying. 'Just ignore them.'

However good the advice, it was impossible for her son to follow. A few days later the crisis reached its peak when Philip ran away from home and lived rough for two days before being found and brought home by the police. It was only then that the extent of his distress was appreciated and steps taken to help him resolve the crisis. The inability of many adults, however loving and well intentioned, to see events through the eyes of a child is responsible for these dismissive reactions, and the often-heard comment that it is 'just a stage he is going through'. Events that once seemed vitally important often pale into insignificance with the passage of time so that, reflecting on past miseries, we can only wonder why on earth we ever got so worked up about them.

The procedures described below not only enable you to discover whether your child is experiencing a life crisis, but also provide a measure of its severity. Pictures can also sometimes be used to identify the precise cause of the crisis. The key sign to look out for is an absence of arms in drawings of the human figure. The link between such an omission and the powerful, but frequently concealed, emotions associated with a life crisis, was first discovered by Dr Francesca Abbele, a research psychologist at the University of Florence. After studying hundreds of drawings made by children – aged from 4 to 12 years – experiencing life crises of varying intensity, Dr Abbele found that arms were omitted from their drawings soon after the traumatic event but returned once the crisis was passed.

Although nobody knows exactly why this happens, a possible explanation may be found in the fact that, for young children, hands and arms are their chief means of exercising control over the outside world and the main method by which control is exercised over them. While other children and adults can usually manipulate people, things and events quite effectively through their use of language, the under-twelves tend to rely far more on physical contact. In early infancy, fingers and hands allow a mysterious world to be cautiously explored and the intense curiosity of the very young to be, at least partially, satisfied. This emphasis on the importance of physical contact declines only slowly as the child grows older. It is often the sense of touch more than any other which provides information about their surroundings. Their own hands and arms reach out to grasp, to hold or throw aside, to destroy or create, to defend or protect while adult hands are a source of both pleasure and pain, of reassurance and restraint. A toddler silently asks to be picked up by raising both arms in mute supplication, an adult strokes away the tears of a miserable child and clasps the hand of a frightened one. It seems reasonable, therefore, to suppose that hands and arms have a far greater significance for young children than they do for older ones.

By omitting them from their pictures the child is expressing the belief that they can no longer exercise control over events in their lives. It is this very lack of control, this growing feeling of helplessness, that lies at the heart of a life crisis.

When Philip was teased unmercifully by his classmates over the birthmark he could see no way of escaping the situation or of preventing their cruelty. He felt himself powerless to prevent their sly jokes or escape the relentless mockery. This link between a childhood life crisis and the absence of arms in figure drawings is clearly illustrated by the series of pictures below. (Illustrations 4a–d).

ILLUSTRATION 4a   ILLUSTRATION 4b

Illustration 4a was drawn by five-year-old Tony a few weeks before his mother gave birth to her new baby. Although both parents tried hard to minimize any jealousy by giving him as much of their time and attention as before, Tony became convinced that his mother had rejected him in favour of the baby.

Illustration 4b was produced, at our request, during the height of Tony's emotional crisis. At this point – three months after the birth – his behaviour had become so troublesome that he and his parents were taking part in family therapy. Notice that the hands and arms have been omitted entirely from the picture.

ILLUSTRATION 4c

ILLUSTRATION 4d

Six months later, with the relationship between Tony and his mother somewhat improved, hands and arms start reappearing in the drawings (see illustrations 4c, 4d), although they are still not featured as prominently as in the pre-crisis pictures, indicating that Tony is still feeling doubtful about his ability to control the situation. Finally, about a year after the crisis occurred, Tony's behaviour has returned to normal and arms have been restored in his pictures.

If you now look back to Chapter 1 and John's paintings, you will see the same features in the picture he made at the peak of his emotional crisis. The intensity of the child's life crisis can be discovered, therefore, from the extent to which hands and arms are missing. The more drawings children produce where these features have been left out, the more intense their emotional distress is likely to be, and the more powerfully are they experiencing a loss of control. The earlier you can identify the crisis by paying close attention to this feature of their pictures, the easier it usually proves to put matters right.

When describing Tania's anxiety about hospitals, we explained that when a particular topic is featured persistently, it becomes very probable that this subject, or some key aspect of it, lies at the root of the trouble. The importance of recurring themes was first recognized by Dr Rose Alshuler, whose other findings have already been described. She discovered that in crisis children will often represent, over and over again, some specific situation, activity, object, animal, person or place. As the crisis deepens they may become so obsessed with the focus of their misery that nothing else is depicted.

Sean, a ten-year-old Irish boy who saw his father shot dead by masked gunmen, became obsessed by firearms. Every picture he created contained at least one weapon, often a pistol, the weapon used in his father's killing. The colours he chose matched the angry and gloomy theme of his subject matter, vivid reds, deep purples and swathes of black. As Sean's emotional crisis peaked he was drawing and painting up to ten pictures a day, all dominated by the theme of guns (see illustration 5).

A similar, though less tragic case, described by Dr Alshuler concerned a child, in her first year at nursery school, whose parents had recently separated. She was consequently shuttled

ILLUSTRATION 5

backwards and forwards between them, spending a few nights in the father's house, then a short time with her mother, then a week or so with various relatives. A recurring theme in this little girl's paintings was a large red shape – it was found in 133 of the 187 pictures she produced over a two-month period. Asked what it represented, she replied:

'This is a house ... this is where I live.' As Dr Alshuler points out, this little girl was obsessed by what life had denied her – a home of her own.

We have looked so far at the link between drawings and the emotional upheavals created by a major life crisis. Considerable distress can also be caused, however, by a wide variety of incidents and activities which are much less obvious and less dramatic than those already described. Dr Hariet Wadeson, a researcher at the Laboratory of Clinical Science at the National Institute of Mental Health in Bethesda, Maryland, has made a major study of the images associated with depression in children. Working with children aged between 6 and 12 years, we have found that the features in drawings and paintings she identified offer an excellent method for identifying and assessing the extent of this negative and damaging emotion.

The depressed child is generally withdrawn, uncommunicative, tearful and reluctant to attempt unfamiliar or even mildly challenging tasks. The motivation of such children is low, and they usually have a poor view of themselves and their chances of achieving anything worthwhile. Such feelings can easily result from seemingly trivial episodes – for example, being scolded or criticized, getting lower than anticipated marks in an examination, taking home a poor end-of-year report, breaking up with a friend, having a crush on a teacher or older child and so on. Recently, however, we have found an increasing number of children, around the ages of 11 and 12, who are deeply depressed about their job prospects after leaving school and who express deep pessimism about the possibility of a nuclear war.

An important clue to depression is the amount of blank space which the child leaves in a drawing. The bleaker their outlook on life, the more empty areas one is likely to find in their pictures. This feature is well illustrated by the pictures produced by Sandra, aged ten (see illustrations 6a and 6b). Both were drawn on the same sized paper and the subject matter is similar in each case. In the four weeks which separated them, however, the little girl had become depressed about her physical appearance after being told that she must wear glasses.

In the first picture the house and tree almost fill the page while the remaining space is taken up by birds, the sun, bushes and so on. A few weeks later Sandra's tree and house had shrunk in size, other details were left out and the picture is conspicuous for its unused areas.

A second easily identifiable feature in the art of depressed children is a greater constriction in the drawing (see illustrations 7a and 7b). The first picture was made by Alex, aged seven, at a time when he was a bright, cheerful boy who faced the future with optimistic good humour. Six months later, after he had been unable to win a scholarship which his older brother had obtained with ease, Alex felt himself a failure. Alex's change in feelings about himself and his abilities was reflected in the cramped drawing style of the second illustration. A comparison between the car in the two pictures makes the differences clear.

A further indication of the child's depression is a loss of organization in their pictures, as illustrations 8a and 8b clearly show. The first was drawn by 11-year-old Adrian before a brief period of mild depression following the death of his grandmother. He drew the second, at our request, during the time he felt so miserable. The differences in the degree of organization and the constriction in the second illustration are obvious.

The final feature to look out for is lack of completeness in pictures made during a bout of depression. The drawings in illustrations 9a and 9b were both made by an eight-year-old girl, the first before and the second during a period when she was feeling rather unhappy. Notice how details of fur and whiskers present in the pre-depression mouse picture are absent from the second drawing, in which the mouse even lacks a well-defined nose. This lack of care and attention to the finer points of pictures is caused by a general slowing-down of physical responses – known as motor retardation – which is a common symptom of even mild depression.

ILLUSTRATION 6a

ILLUSTRATION 6b

ILLUSTRATION 7a

ILLUSTRATION 7b

ILLUSTRATION 8a

ILLUSTRATION 8b

ILLUSTRATION 9a

ILLUSTRATION 9b

If only one of these features appears in your child's paintings or drawings on a few occasions, it probably reflects only a passing unhappiness. When two or more occur fairly frequently, however, it is time to try to discover what is causing their depression. Once you have been alerted to the fact that a negative emotion such as depression or excessive anxiety is being felt it may only take some sensitive questioning and, even more importantly, careful listening to identify the source of these feelings. You can then start working with your child either to resolve the problem or, if this proves impossible, to help make a particular situation more tolerable.

As we have seen, personality factors help determine the way children behave towards others and these relationships are often the cause of powerful emotional responses which may either help or hinder their social growth. It is, therefore, very helpful to understand the precise nature of these relationships in order to appreciate the influence being exerted over them by friends and family. In Chapter 7 we explain how picture analysis can help you achieve such an understanding by revealing what children really feel about their companions, their brothers or sisters and you, their parents.

CHAPTER SEVEN

What pictures reveal about friendships

Mary, aged eleven, insists that Samantha is her dearest friend, yet seldom wants to play with her. How does she really feel about their friendship?

Nine-year-old Simon assures his parents that he likes his English teacher, yet he seems to be especially anxious on days when that subject is on the timetable. Is he being honest about his feelings or hiding the fact that this master makes him anxious?

At first Paul seemed to get on well with his adopted sister. Recently, however, he has become moody and withdrawn. How can his parents discover their son's true feelings?

Relationships, like other important aspects of a child's world, are often hard to understand. This is not really so surprising when you consider the numerous barriers to insight which can arise within even the most affectionate family. Firstly, many children feel a great reluctance to talk about their feelings for others, and secondly, even when they would like to discuss their relationships openly, they find it hard to put their sentiments into words. Ask the average child what he likes about his constant companion, for instance, and you are liable to get a puzzled frown, followed by some general comment such as: 'He's good fun ...' 'She makes me laugh ...' or 'He's OK, I suppose ...'. Even the depth of feelings aroused by a greatly disliked youngster is unlikely to produce much more information than: 'He's horrible ...' or 'I hate him ...'

Children's friendships tend, furthermore, to be rather volatile. Although a particular child may have one or two firm friends, others drift in and out of favour. A boy who has been another's constant companion for weeks suddenly falls out of favour and becomes a bitter foe. A few days later the upset is forgotten and the friendship restored. When we look at relationships between children and adults, the picture becomes even more confusing and confused. Children may feel threatened by a teacher who is convinced that he or she is well liked by that child. Parents are often so certain that their children will continue to love them in spite of everything that they never pause to reflect on how the child may view their behaviour.

In order to help children acquire essential social skills and build the self-confidence needed to seek out and develop relationships, it is important to gain a clear perspective on their views of others – adults as well as children, family as well as friends – and this picture analysis can do. This is because, in spontaneously creating images, the child often expresses emotional responses to others that lie beyond language and, sometimes, beyond their conscious awareness. In this chapter we look at some of these images, explaining what they reveal about your child's relationships with brothers or sisters, friends and fellow students, relatives, teachers and parents.

Picturing friends and foes

Is it possible to tell whether a child likes or dislikes somebody from the way they draw them?

That was the intriguing question which Dr Gary Gilbert, at Kansas State University, set out to answer by studying the pictures and friendships of a large group of 12-year-old schoolchildren. Dr Gilbert asked his young artists to draw pictures of people they knew and then say how much each person was liked or disliked. As a result of this revealing study Gary Gilbert was able to pinpoint three features in children's drawings which clearly distinguish friends from foes. By looking out for the same signs, you can accurately establish the real nature of your child's relationships. The signs to watch for are:

When a child pictures somebody he or she dislikes, far fewer details are included than when drawing a portrait of a friend. Illustration 1 shows ten-year-old Simon's English teacher and its lack of detail contradicts his assertion that he likes the man. As you can see, the hands have been left out almost entirely, while the clothes are simply sketched in.

These omissions are all the more striking when compared with Simon's picture of his games teacher (see illustration 2). Her features include pupils in the eyes and eyelashes, nostrils, hair and fingernails. There are buttons on her tracksuit, her belt has a buckle and adjustment holes. She is wearing shoes with laces, lace holes and rubber soles. Simon told us that this teacher was the 'best person in my school'.

The second feature to look out for is sometimes rather more subtle. Dr Gilbert found that when drawing somebody they disliked, children tended to use more angles and fewer curves. These differences are clearly shown in the pictures (see illustrations 3 and 4), made for us on the same day by nine-year-old Arthur. The first is of Mike, Arthur's best friend in class. The second shows Jim, the boy's woodwork master, somebody he actively disliked and feared. Notice how Mike is drawn using a large number of curves, while Jim is created almost entirely out of straight lines and sharp angles. The head is a rectangle, finger-tips are squared off, the hat becomes an extension of the head and the boots look like boxes. There are few details on either the face or the clothing.

In the original, Jim's clothes are bright red, his face a garish pink while the bow-tie, boots and hat were all black, colours associated with aggression and unhappiness. At first Arthur was reluctant to talk about Jim, other than saying casually: 'He's OK I suppose...'. But, because the signs of dislike and hostility were so obvious, we came back to their relationship several times during the discussion and, finally, Arthur admitted miserably: 'If you really want to know I hate him... he's always picking on me.'

The last sign of dislike to look for is a lack of organization in the picture. The greater its disorganization the less the person depicted is liked.

Illustrations 5 and 6 were drawn by seven-year-old Tamsin.

The first shows Sandy, her sister, of whom she was very fond, and the second Rachel, a hated cousin. You will notice that, when drawing her cousin, Tamsin made little attempt to impose order on her picture. The girl's arms seem to be misplaced and the legs are out of proportion with the body. This is not due to lack of skill, however, since Tamsin has drawn her sister far more accurately.

We selected these illustrations because they offer such vivid examples of the key features under discussion. While you may not always find them represented so clearly and graphically in all your child's drawings, they will certainly be present to some extent in any pictures of people who are either much liked or greatly disliked. You should also take into account the colour choice for clothing since, as we explained in the last chapter, these preferences tell us a great deal about your child's emotional response.

Assessing your child's relationships

Provide your child with several sheets of paper, pencils, crayons or paint, and ensure that a wide variety of colours are available so that any preferences are due to free choice rather than a lack of alternatives. Ask the child to produce paintings of two people whom you know for certain are very well liked. These can then be used as the basis for comparison when assessing other pictures. Now get your child to draw and paint a range of pictures which explore any relationships you are interested in assessing. Needless to say these should not all be done on the same day or boredom may bias the results – two or three is usually the maximum per session, although this will depend on the child's age and their enthusiasm for painting. Make certain that each drawing is clearly identified with the subject's name and always remember to compliment your child on his or her drawing ability at the end of each session.

Start by comparing each picture with the first two paintings of a well-liked person. Notice any differences in fine detail included on face, body and clothing. Look out for angles used in preference to curves, particularly in drawings of the head, shoulders, hands and feet. Finally, consider how well or-ganized the drawings are: have the legs and arms been drawn

ILLUSTRATION 1

english
teacher.

ILLUSTRATION 2

GAMES TEACHER

ILLUSTRATION 3

ILLUSTRATION 4

ILLUSTRATION 5

ILLUSTRATION 6

in proportion, or does any significant distortion exist in the shape of trunk or limbs? Use your two comparison drawings and the chart below to rate each painting in terms of like or dislike.

Points for comparison

Amount of detail	*Rating*
Considerably less	− 2
Somewhat less	− 1
About the same	0
Slightly more	+ 1
Much greater	+ 2

Straight lines and angles	
Many more	− 2
A few more	− 1
About the same number	0
Slightly fewer	+ 1
Far fewer	+ 2

Degree of organization	
Much less	− 2
Somewhat less	− 1
About the same	0
Rather more	+ 1
Much more	+ 2

After adding the score for each picture you can rank each subject most liked to least liked. The higher a positive score the more that person is liked, and, correspondingly, the greater the negative score the more he or she is disliked. This analysis can produce some fascinating insights into your child's friends and foes, both children and adults. You can find out which of their companions are truly liked, which are tolerated and which ones are regarded with hostility. The same assessments can be made about relatives, family friends and the child's teachers.

In many cases you will obtain information that could not be gained in any other way. Even children who are sufficiently articulate and self-confident to talk freely about youngsters of their own age may fall silent when asked to express an opinion about adults, especially authority figures. They may fear retribution, or punishment for impertinence, if they tell you what they really think. Less forthcoming children will often find it impossible even to talk about feelings towards close friends, let alone those who make them anxious or unhappy. Often just thinking about such individuals can create distress and a desire to avoid dwelling on the topic any longer than necessary.

Assessing family portraits

Drawings can also be used to assess a child's feelings not only for individual members of the family, but for the family as a whole.

In a comfortably furnished office at New York's Mount Sinai Hospital in New York City, a ten-year-old boy is drawing a picture of his parents, his brothers and sisters, his grandmother, uncle and aunt. He is not attending a painting class, or taking part in art therapy. Instead, the family portrait will be used by psychologist Dr Wilfred Hulse to analyse relationships within the home. Over the past few years, he has found that this simple *Family drawing test*, provides an extremely effective method of exploring children's most intimate and significant relationships.

Almost all the drawings Dr Hulse has studied provide strong evidence of conflicts between one or more members of the family. Such conflicts are not necessarily abnormal, however, since almost all children find themselves at odds with their father or mother, brothers or sisters, from time to time. Where such a conflict is intense and persistent, however, steps should be taken to identify and eliminate the root cause of the problems. If allowed to continue they are likely to undermine emotional health, inhibit contructive discussion between those involved and damage other relationships within the home. The father and son who are at loggerheads, for example, may do little except exchange hurtful remarks as their feelings for one another become increasingly negative. At the same time the wife and other children may feel obliged to take sides, so dividing the family and extending the conflict.

Conflict is revealed in the child's picture by the following key features:

Rivalry is indicated if a child fails to draw in the arms and legs when picturing his brothers or sisters. Illustration 7, by six-year-old Susie, shows her brother Bobbie, aged ten, and five-year-old sister, Jeanie. Susie worships her older brother, but regards Jeanie as a rival for her parents' affection. These feelings reveal themselves in the fact that while Bobbie has his arms and hands drawn in accurate detail, Jeanie's have been left out.

ILLUSTRATION 7

Dominance within a family is revealed by the way a child draws the different figures. In illustration 8 nine-year-old Richard depicts his father standing, and clearly giving orders, while he and his mother are seated and listening. This dominant stance shows that the boy sees the man as exerting the greatest authority over the family. You can see the same posture in the second of John's drawings of his stepfather (see Chapter 1).

In general the parent seen as wielding the most power will be shown in such a way that he, or she, contrives to dominate the picture, sometimes through the use of different postures, as in Richard's painting, or by being drawn taller, larger and more impressive looking than anybody else present.

ILLUSTRATION 8

ILLUSTRATION 9

The next sign to look for involves the use of the background and foreground, and can only be found in the art of children whose skill is sufficient for them to understand and use perspective. Notice how, in illustration 9, 11-year-old Vicki places herself in the background while her brother Paul, aged eight, stands in the foreground. Despite being older than Paul, Vicki has felt inferior to him. She has judged herself fairly plain, while he is a strikingly handsome child.

Vicki, who is rather shy and reserved, has found it hard to make many friends, but her brother, a gregarious and socially skilled child, has had little difficulty. These feelings of insignificance are clearly mirrored in the way she has represented her position in the drawing. Similar conclusions can be drawn about a child's feelings towards his parents. If the father is in the background, for example, and the mother is in the foreground, it indicates that the child sees her as the more dominant marriage partner.

The final sign to look for is that of relative distance between the figures in the drawings. Illustration 10, drawn by nine-

ILLUSTRATION 10

year-old Tim, shows him with his parents and ten-year-old brother Simon. The boy places himself, his brother and mother close together, while his father is some distance to their right. Simon has his hand on Tim's shoulder and their mother seems to be reaching out to make contact with her son. The man, by comparison, almost appears to be part of a different picture, indeed he is only just on the drawing paper.

The year before this drawing was made, Tim's parents had separated for a time. Although they were living together again, Tim's mother disliked her husband, a cold, sarcastic man. Tim and Simon took their mother's side in every dispute, so the family had virtually split into two warring factions. Both parents were convinced, despite their frequent arguments, that the boys regarded their marriage as happy. They also insisted that Tim and Simon were extremely fond of their father, and would have been very distressed if they were to separate. Tim's portrait of the family reveals a very different situation.

You can expand on insights which the pictures provide, by asking the following questions:

What are the people in the picture doing?

What are the people in the picture saying?

What will the people in the picture do next?

What will the people in the picture say next?

These usually suffice to identify exactly which emotions are being reflected in the pictures. When, by using these questions, we explored the feelings which Tim had revealed in his painting, he replied that his father had just come home from the office and was angry because supper was late: 'When he's through with telling Mum off, he'll be on to me for not doing better at school,' he explained. 'Then he'll go and watch telly in the other room while Mum takes it out on us. I'll go up to my room and read.'

If you want to explore this aspect of your child's relationships, simply ask him or her to draw the family. Make it clear that you want a portrait which includes everybody, perhaps by

saying something along these lines:
'I'd like you to paint a picture of the family, which shows us all either at home or outdoors. There's no hurry, but you must try not to leave anybody out.' When the picture is finished, congratulate your child and then ask the four questions above.

We have looked so far at relationships between your child and other individuals, and the ways in which family feelings can be revealed. Pictures also allow us to assess how well or how badly a child gets on with other people, both other children and adults. Dr Alan Paul, of Harvard University, and his co-worker Dr Rachel Hare, of Wellesley College, carried out an extensive study on a sample of 166 children, aged six to ten, which established the accuracy and reliability of an assessment procedure which they called simply the *Draw a group test.*

They began by asking form teachers to rate every child in terms of leadership skills or social isolation. Which children, they wondered, were most likely to invent games, cooperate with others on group tasks, and take the lead in a team activity. At the other end of the ranking, which of the children were followers rather than leaders, which of them joined in the least and most often chose to remain on the sidelines. When the same children were later asked to draw themselves playing with others, a significant link was found between social isolation and the pictures produced. As in the family portraits, the relative sizes of the figures in the drawings provide an important clue about their significance in the child's life. An equally significant feature is the size of the child himself, or herself, in relation to their playmates.

Philip, aged nine, told us that he is the small figure in the foreground of illustration 11. Although he at first denied being lonely or feeling frightened of other children, it became obvious over a series of interviews that he was extremely nervous of group activities and disliked having to take part in any type of games. Philip was a lonely little boy, lacking in social skills and very under-confident in his dealings with others.

The smaller the subject draws himself/herself in relation to others in the picture, the poorer their leadership qualities and the greater their feelings of isolation. Leadership is also revealed by how many other children are included in the

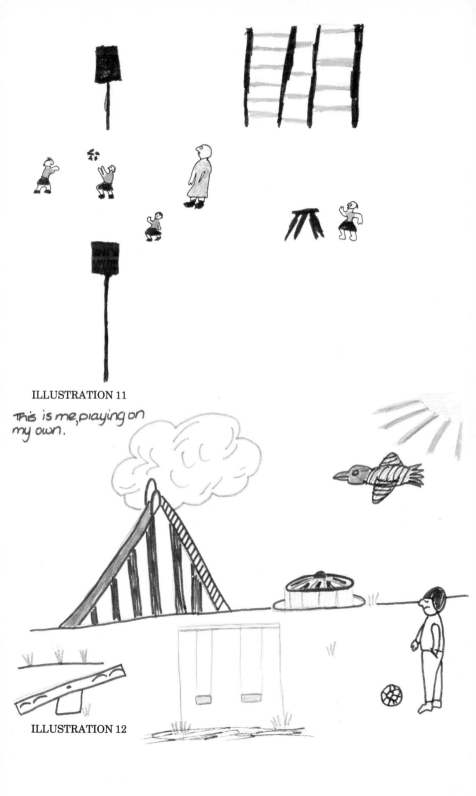

ILLUSTRATION 11

This is me, playing on
my own.

ILLUSTRATION 12

picture. The more there are, the more likely it is that the child sees himself/herself as being a leader rather than a follower.

Children who regularly draw playground scenes in which they are either all alone or with just a few companions are almost certainly just as isolated in real life. The solitary little figure in the deserted playground in illustration 12 is the artist, 12-year-old Miguel. Its poignant caption reads: 'This is me, playing on my own.'

The third sign of isolation to look for is the inclusion of authority figures, teachers, policemen, and adults obviously involved in supervising activities. The final feature to watch out for is the distance between the figure representing the subject and the centre of the picture. George, aged ten, is the accepted leader of a group of boys. In his painting, in illustration 13, he is placed right in the middle of the playground activities. Compare this with the drawing in illustration 14 by 8-year-old David, a lonely child who never seemed able to get others to play with him. He has positioned himself on the fringes of the group, reflecting the isolation he undoubtedly feels in everyday life.

ILLUSTRATION 13

ILLUSTRATION 14

To carry out this simple but important assessment on your own child, provide drawing materials and say something along these lines:
'Think of the children you would most like to play with. Imagine the kind of games you really enjoy playing and then paint the scene for me. I want you to be sure to include yourself somewhere in the picture.'
As with the previous assessment, you can obtain further important insights by asking the right kind of questions while looking at the picture:

What are the people in the picture doing right now?

What are they going to do?

What are the people in the picture saying?

What are they going to say?

Are you happy or sad in this picture?

You should also investigate any unusual features of the picture. When we asked Miguel where all the other children had gone, in his playground picture, he replied:
'They didn't want to play with me ... they don't like me very much.'

Having assessed your child's feelings towards others, you may be cheered to find there are no major conflicts or serious difficulties and that he or she appears to relate well to both friends and relatives. On the other hand you might discover that there are difficulties, at school, in the family or in the child's ability to develop friendships. In this case you will certainly want to know how best such difficulties can be overcome. Chapter 8 explains how to help children who experience problems in this area. If your own child does not require such assistance you may prefer to go to Chapter 10 in which we describe how pictures can be used to assess your child's level of creativity.

CHAPTER EIGHT

Helping your child to make friends

Research has shown that children tend to exaggerate feelings of isolation and loneliness in their pictures. This is especially true of the introverted child who, as we have seen, tends to take a somewhat more pessimistic view of life than most. Far from being a weakness in assessment technique, however, this exaggeration is one of its greatest advantages. By slightly amplifying the extent of such problems, picture analysis makes them easier to identify at an early stage and, as a result, much simpler to solve. The danger, of course, is that adults will become so alarmed by the discovery that their child has some difficulty in making friends that they embark on some hasty action.

If your assessment suggests that your child may be having difficulty in forming relationships, and could be feeling lonely or rejected as a result, you must first make certain that the signs you have observed occur consistently over a period of days or even weeks. A passing sadness, perhaps caused by a temporary rejection, can sometimes produce these features in a child's pictures. At the same time, it would be wise to take stock of your child's relationships, so that if it becomes necessary to bring about any changes you will have a better idea how and where to start. Practical procedures for improving the situation are described below, but let's start by looking at the kind of problems which can occur inside the family circle.

Family feelings

You can very often resolve conflicts and difficulties in the family fairly quickly and easily once their presence has been detected. A child whose pictures reveal a rivalry, for example, with a brother or sister might be helped by the parent finding out what has caused these feelings and then trying to put matters right. When deciding on your plan of action, bear in mind the knowledge gained by analysing your child's personality, as these factors exert a powerful influence over the child's responses. Take, for instance, an extremely sensitive child who may be masking his true feelings by displays of apathy or indifference, attitudes which – not surprisingly – lead you to favour the other children who are more rewarding to deal with.

To reduce conflict and anxiety within the family, you should:

Encourage children to be open and frank when talking about their feelings for one another.

Not be afraid to express your own emotions.

Allow each child to express his, or her, individuality and do not try to mould the child's personality to satisfy your own needs or expectations.

How to help lonely children

When a child is lonely, unwilling to take part in group activities, and unable to make or sustain friendships, it takes more than kind words and good intentions to overcome their isolation. Our research suggests there are three types of child who have difficulties in developing lasting relationships.

The Refuser
Remains on the sidelines when others are playing together and seldom joins in unless forced to do so.

The Incompetent
Tries to join in but never appears to be made especially welcome by other children, is unable to make friends easily and lacks the confidence to risk taking a chance on rejection.

The Bully

Unlike the refuser and the incompetent, the bully involves himself all too vigorously with other children. Attempts to become part of a group are characterized by aggression and hostility, which makes them feared and avoided.

In many cases it is possible to identify the most appropriate category by observing the child's reactions while playing. There will be occasions, however, when the situation is complicated by the child switching from one type of behaviour to another. The refuser, having rejected advances from other children and resisted adult attempts to persuade him or her to join in a game suddenly makes a determined, but perhaps ineffectual, effort to do so. The incompetent, frustrated by a lack of success in some game, resorts to bullying. The bully may be so intimidated by the response of adults that he withdraws completely and becomes a refuser.

The personality of the child plays a large part in determining which strategy is adopted. Introverted, very sensitive children – especially if they also have a low energy focus – are likely to withdraw and become refusers. Extravert, high energy focus, low sensitivity children are more likely to turn to bullying if their attempts to make friends and influence others by peaceful means prove unsuccessful. The kind of help you should provide will vary according to the basic needs of each child. Assess these using picture analysis, calm questioning about the content of their drawings and your personal observations of their behaviour.

Helping the refuser child

In almost any group of children you will find one or two who are the wallflowers of the playground. They hang around the fringes of any game, looking on but seldom either joining in or being asked to take part by others. To discover why this happens and how to help, we first have to appreciate the concept of *reinforcement* in establishing ways of behaving. In everyday terms this simply means that if an activity is followed by a reward, it is more likely to be repeated. If, on the other hand, the activity is punished, it is less likely to occur again.

The punishments which children may encounter while playing with others include rejection, and perhaps physical pain if the game gets too rough. The major penalty exacted from the socially inadequate youngster, however, is acute anxiety: the very thought of having to join in a game or take part in a group activity is sufficient to make them feel mentally and physically distressed. The only way they can see to reduce these extremely unpleasant feelings is by refusing to take part. Once their refusal has been accepted and they are left alone, the fear subsides. This produces the reward which makes it more likely that refusal, rather than acceptance, will be their response on future occasions. The penalty paid, apart from social isolation, is never acquiring the skills needed to play effectively. Their lack of ability makes them incompetent at sports and uninterested when it comes to games. As a result they are less likely to be asked to take part in the future. On those rare occasions when some effort is made to join in, their confidence is further diminished and their anxiety increased by an almost inevitable failure.

One of the most usual ways in which parents and teachers attempt to help isolated children involves applying pressure to the child himself, or herself, to join in. This can either take the form of friendly persuasion:
'Oh, do play with John and Mary, they are having so much fun,' or it may be a straight command: 'You can't hang around in school during the break, go out and play with the others.'

The alternative approach is to try to persuade a group of children to welcome the refuser into their game:
'Won't you let Jimmy play with you? He looks so sad. . .'
'Why not give Mary a chance to join in now. She's only waiting to be asked. . .' Although the others may agree, under protest, they are hardly likely to welcome the newcomer with much enthusiasm and he or she may be confronted by thinly disguised hostility and plaintive protests, all of which make the unfortunate child even more unhappy and unwilling to join in.

The lesson learned by both these adult interventions, therefore, is that playing with other children is an unpleasant and unrewarding experience. It quite often happens that children who refuse to take part in games or sports do so because they do not understand the rules of the game. Part of their anxiety stems from the fear of making a fool of themselves and being rejected by the others. To overcome this unhelpful situation, you need the cooperation of two or three children of about the same age as the child with difficulties. Begin with small groups of the refuser child plus two or three other children. Avoid selecting youngsters who are especially dominant or even slightly aggressive, since this will obviously make the anxious refuser extremely unhappy. If you know any other parents whose own children tend not to join in successfully, then it might be possible to form a group using other refusers.

Create a play session in which cooperation is essential to success and enjoyment. Avoid any games which have a competitive element, either between individual children or different teams. Outdoor activities might include setting up a camp, constructing a bridge across a stream, or building a treehouse. For indoor sessions use constructional toys, train sets, car races and so on. All that matters is that the game requires each child to help the other. Encourage the children to take turns, to share, to offer suggestions and to assume responsibility for different parts of the task. Encourage them to talk to one another, to ask each other questions, to share information, to offer praise for a good idea and to provide mutual support when things go wrong. Although you will have to set up the games and start the activity going, limit your role to a minimum as soon as you can by encouraging each child to assume responsibilities.

Helping the incompetent child

Any child who tries to play with others but consistently fails is well on their way to becoming socially isolated. As with the refuser the underlying problem is a lack of play skills. The idea that young children ever have to learn anything apparently so natural and spontaneous as making friends and playing games may strike you as strange, but the fact is that both are highly skilled social activities with their own sets of rules and unwritten codes of behaviour. The child who has never mastered these skills will be very much in the position of a stranger in a strange land, constantly stumbling into embarrassing error and never being fully accepted by those well versed in the local customs. Even where play involves such apparently unstructured activities as running around or acting out fantasies, considerable learning is necessary in order to join in successfully. The popular child is one who can either think up exciting games or is willing to join in enthusiastically with another's games. By never remaining long enough in any group to acquire these skills, the incompetent child is doomed to remain for ever an outsider.

It is not only introverted children who are found in this category. Extraverts may prove too boisterous for the others to tolerate, while midiverts – as we explained in Chapter 4 – may feel themselves to be outsiders if the others are highly extraverted or very introverted. As with the refuser, the answer lies in teaching the child how to play effectively during special 'training' sessions. Working with a small group of children, start to build self-confidence while helping in the mastery of specific play skills. Encourage sharing, cooperation, amicable discussion, and free exchange of ideas.

For older children knowledge of some sport is often the secret of success in group activities. Children who are poorly coordinated or small in size are often excluded from team games and so never acquire the ability to play them well. Teaching a child how to play, and more importantly how to enjoy, a particular sport is especially helpful. Not all children like team games and there is no reason to force such a choice on them. There are plenty of other activities, such as swimming, cycling, tennis, squash, golf or judo, which children can enjoy in the company of others and so make friends with a shared interest. Parents often assume that schools will teach them all they need to know about sports, but this is not always the case. Personal coaching, help and encouragement can make all the difference to reducing anxiety while building skills and confidence in the uncertain child. Parents with a love for a particular sport will sometimes insist that the child learns to play and enjoy it to an equal extent. We emphasize again the fundamental need to treat all children as individuals with their own unique likes and dislikes, abilities, aptitudes and interests. Give the child the opportunity to learn and enjoy your favourite sport by all means, but do not become irritated or uninterested if they fail to respond as expected.

Parents primarily interested in classroom achievement sometimes assume that activities which do not directly enhance classroom attainment are a waste of time and effort. This is a shortsighted view since physical activity not only keeps children healthy but also helps them to acquire many important social skills.

Helping the bully

Few children provoke adults to anger so quickly and easily as the bully, who is usually a deeply unhappy and often anxious child unable to cope with social challenges and so resorts to aggression.

Punishment from grown-ups, a frequent fate of children given to bullying, does little to eliminate or even reduce their aggressive behaviour. They simply become more cunning about when and where they assault smaller and weaker children. This is because, although the punishment is unpleasant, the immediate rewards of bullying are often agreeable. The bully can, for example, oblige other children to let him or her take over an enjoyable game, commandeer a favourite toy, and achieve a status in the group which he or she might not attain in any other way. Bullying cannot be allowed to continue, of course, because it disrupts the group, making already anxious youngsters even more fearful while provoking self-confident and dominant children to equally aggressive retaliation.

Instead of punishing the bully, adults should try to adopt a more objective approach, discovering first the exact circumstances in which bullying occurs, and so the rewards gained by such behaviour. This will provide insight into the type of situations which make the child feel especially anxious or inadequate. Keep a diary over a period of a week to ten days and note down every occasion on which the child uses bullying to get his own way. On the basis of this knowledge you should then tackle the problem in one of two ways.

First, start building the child's repertoire of skilled social behaviours using the procedures described above. At the same time try to discover and resolve any emotional conflicts which may be producing the aggression.

While providing the child with social skills, it is necessary to remove the rewards of bullying. This can be done by gently, but firmly, removing the child from the group and placing him in surroundings which offer a minimum amount of stimulation. Choose a room with a door which can be locked. This must not be a frightening place, a gloomy cellar or a dark attic, for example, because the idea is not to punish the child in any way: it is to eliminate the reinforcement which was previously being obtained from the aggression. A spare bedroom is ideal but there should be no toys or books, nothing to write with and nothing to listen to or watch. When the child is in this room do not criticize or scold. You should keep your expression and voice as neutral as possible. This is important because, for some bullies, part of their reward is adult attention – even though that attention is punishing. By acting in a neutral manner and by placing the child, for no more than four or five minutes, in a non-rewarding environment it becomes possible to break the link between behaviour and reward.

Warn the child beforehand what will happen if he or she continues to bully, and use this tactic if disobedience continues. You should be prepared for the possibility of an increase in bullying over the first few days as the child tries to recover the previous rewards by stepping up his or her aggression. It is rather like adults shouting to make themselves heard after finding that nobody listens if they talk in a normal voice. If this should happen you must continue to use the procedure – known as *Time-Out* – since if you give in the child will have learned that he can win simply by becoming increasingly aggressive. Far from reducing the bullying you may actually have made matters worse!

There is something of a paradox in helping socially isolated children. The behaviour which has led to their lack of friends and inability to form relationships can itself make adults unwilling to help them learn more successful ways of responding to others. Parents and teachers sometimes become irritated by the child's apparent lack of interest in others, their ineffectual attempts to join in and, especially, their hostility. Helping them to break free from this trap often requires considerable patience and understanding on your part. But, without such guidance, they may grow through a lonely childhood into men and women who will never be able to master the complex, but essential, art of making friends and forming relationships.

CHAPTER NINE

How pictures reveal impulsivity

Maurice and Kirsty are self-assured, sociable, eight-year-olds of above average intelligence. Their behaviour at home and at school, however is very different. Maurice is an impulsive child who tends to speak and act without pausing for thought or reflection. He is rather accident-prone, and not very successful in activities which demand accurate control over bodily movements – such as ball games, gymnastics or dancing. Kirsty is far more thoughtful. When asked a question or presented with a problem she pauses to reflect, and so gives her brain a better chance of coming up with the correct answer. She moves gracefully, seldom drops or breaks things, paints, draws and writes carefully, and is top of her dancing class.

These differences in attitude and ability naturally cause adults to form very different opinions about the two children. Teachers regard Kirsty as being brighter and less extravert than Maurice, while even the boy's parents were surprised when picture analysis revealed their son to be both more intelligent and more introverted than they had imagined. As we saw in Chapter 4, extravert children do tend to think and act more impulsively than introverts, while there was no denying that in terms of classroom successes, Kirsty outshone Maurice. If personality and IQ differences were not the cause of their behaviour, what was responsible? The key influence, it turns out, lies in the temperamental factor of impulsivity. If you have been puzzled by the fact that, although your own child often behaves impulsively, he did not score high on the extravert assessment, the same explanation may hold true here as well.

How the impulsive child responds

As one would expect, impulsive children usually speak and act without giving much thought to what they say and do. They blurt out remarks, jump in at the deep end, embark on projects without thinking them through, and generally show a quick reaction to events in their life. A child who does his school work in an impulsive manner is likely to overlook important factors, leave out vital details and make careless errors, and may well write messily. When playing games or sports such children are accident-prone and lack the discipline essential to team efforts.

How the reflective child responds

The reflective student is cautious and likes to think hard before making decisions, coming up with answers or embarking on a particular course of action. Such children pay attention to details and are less prone to careless errors. In play and sports they are less likely to have accidents and are more disciplined members of a team. Their writing and drawing is usually neat and orderly. They organize their work schedules with precision and are tidy in their appearance. Highly reflective children are often paragons of scholastic virtue. It will therefore come as no surprise, especially to teachers, to learn that only a small minority of youngsters can be classed as highly reflective, just as most children avoid the extremes of impulsivity.

Because impulsivity can exert such a powerful influence over a child's behaviour and attainments, it is very helpful for parents and teachers to be able to assess this aspect of temperament as accurately and as objectively as possible. As a result of extensive research by Professor Max Holt at the University of Detroit, such an assessment can now be carried out by means of a drawing test.

Making the assessment

Your child should be sitting comfortably with drawing

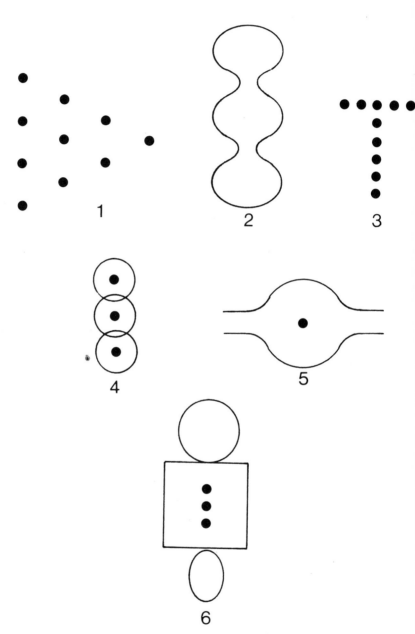

1

2

3

4

5

6

ILLUSTRATION 1

materials to hand so that he or she can start work as soon as you give the word. All you need do is show your child the six designs in illustration 1, starting with number 1 and working through, in sequence, to number 6. Cover all but the first design and ask your child to study it carefully and not to start drawing until you say. Count slowly to five, then cover the design and tell him to draw it from memory.

Repeat the process for the remaining designs, making certain that, while showing a particular figure, the others remain covered. There is no time limit on the assessment, but all the copies must be completed in one session.

Scoring the results

Professor Holt identified five types of distortion which, when present in any of the copies, provide a reliable indication of impulsivity. The more distortions there are, the more impulsive the child who drew them.

Sign one

Start by studying the copies to see whether there are any straight or angled lines where curves should be, as in illustration 2. The child intended this to be a copy of Design 2 on the original test which, as you can see, contains neither straight lines nor angles.

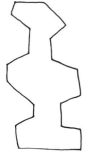

ILLUSTRATION 2   ILLUSTRATION 3

Sign two

Loops instead of circles. Illustration 3 was supposed to represent Design 6 on the test. Notice the loop at the top of the child's drawing which has replaced the circle on the original design.

Sign three
Circles for dots or dots for circles. Notice how, in the copy of the first design (illustration 4), only three of the circles are copied accurately, the remainder having been replaced with dots.

Sign four
Dashes where dots should have been. Illustration 5 is an impulsive child's version of Design 3 on the original test. As you can see almost all the dots have been transformed into dashes.

Sign five
The addition of loops, curlicues or other embellishments not present in the original. Illustration 6 is a child's copy from memory of Design 4. Notice the extra ornamentation, added to the middle of the circles, which replaces the three dots on the original.

ILLUSTRATION 4   ILLUSTRATION 5   ILLUSTRATION 6

Examine each drawing in turn to see whether Sign One is present in any of them. The only copy where this cannot occur is Design 3. Now look at all those containing this sign and work out whether it occurs in more or less than half the child's version. Where the first sign is found in more than 50 per cent of the child's drawing, award that sign two points. If the sign occurs in less than 50 per cent of the copy award one point. When the sign is absent there is no score. For example, compare the copy made by a child (illustration 7) with the original of Design 1. As you can see straight lines and angles have been used throughout, so this scores 2 points. In the second version (illustration 8), however, a second child has used lines and angles in only about half the copy, which scores 1 point as a result.

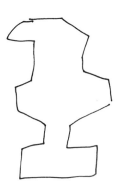

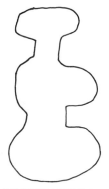

ILLUSTRATION 7   ILLUSTRATION 8

After going through all six copies looking for Sign One, move to Sign Two, and score each of the child's drawings in the same manner. Repeat this process for all six copies.

Remember:
Sign not present at all = 0 points
Sign present in less than half the image = 1 point
Sign present in more than half the image = 2 points

Total the points (the maximum possible score is 60) and use the chart below to assess the child's rating on the impulsivity-reflectivity scale.

Score	*Age of child*				
	4 – 5	6 – 7	8 – 9	10 – 11	12+
0 – 5	R	R	R	R	R
6 – 10	R	R	R	R	A
11 – 15	R	R	R	A	A
16 – 20	A	A	A	A	A
21 – 30	A	A	A	I	I
31 – 40	A	A	I	I	I
41 – 50	I	I	I	I	I
51 – 60	I	I	I	I	I

Find your child's score on the left of the chart. Now move to the right until you arrive at the column which contains your child's age. Here you will find one of three letters – I, A or R. If your child has obtained an I, it means he or she is more impulsive than other children. An A indicates your child is average on impulsivity. An R tells you that your child is more reflective than other children.

How the test works

Drawing straight lines requires less effort than creating the carefully formed curves in the moderately complex designs included in the test. Because impulsive children tend to take the most direct route, and as a straight line is the shortest distance between two points, these are preferred to curves. A desire to cut corners, also a feature of the impulsive child's attitude to life, causes them to use angles rather than curves.

The same explanation applies to the substitution of loops for circles, since it is much easier to produce a quick, carelessly formed loop than to try and draw a carefully formed circle. The replacement of circles by dots and dots by circles (Sign Three) is likely to reflect impulsivity at the stage where the original design is being studied before a copy is attempted. Instead of paying careful attention to each feature of the drawing, an impulsive youngster gives it no more than a rapid glance. The same explanation applies to Sign Four where the child draws dashes where dots ought to be.

What is it likely to mean if your child has scored either an I or an R on this assessment? We have already described some of the more obvious ways in which impulsive and reflective children will differ and considered how their behaviour affects a wide range of activities. Research has shown, however, that these fundamental and inborn differences carry wider implications for performance and attainment than so far considered.

How impulsive children respond

The fact that impulsive youngsters generally act on impulse means that they are very much influenced by passing moods and not very good at planning ahead or making provisions for the future. The ease with which they can be distracted from the task at hand makes it difficult for them to concentrate for long.

Although they may attend part of the time, anything slightly unusual or unexpected instantly diverts them. An impulsive child's attention to the teacher, for example, will rapidly switch to watching others playing outside the classroom window or listening to a commotion in the corridor.

Although impulsivity is unrelated to a child's level of intelligence, impulsive children – like Maurice – are often assessed as having a lower IQ. Their inability to concentrate makes it hard for them to keep up with lessons and make sense of what they are being taught. This lack of knowledge, compounded by their hasty and often ill-considered answers, results in poor marks. Furthermore, the impulsive youngster's less precise muscle control often results in untidy and illegible handwriting. Since both teachers, and parents, tend to equate good marks and neat handwriting with a high IQ, the misjudgment is hardly surprising.

An important component of success in any intellectually demanding task is the ability to attend selectively to just one part of the available information and deal with this before moving to the next step. In order to solve the equation: $2x + 4 = 6x - 8$, for example, the child must first focus his or her attention on the numbers associated with an x and bring them to the same side of the equation. Unless this is done questions like this cannot be solved. Similarly, accurate reading and writing requires a precise focus of attention on the letters being written and the words being spoken. Research has shown that impulsive children find it much harder to direct their thoughts in this way. Given a complex design to copy, for example, they will make some errors simply through not having focused their attention clearly enough on the original. This failure causes them to make foolish mistakes in arithmetic, reading and writing.

In sports and games, impulsive children often move swiftly and make rapid decisions. This general display of speed is accompanied, however, by an overall lack of precision and many errors of judgment which undermine the overall performance. When playing casually, the impulsive child is more likely to have accidents which are often seen by adults as the result of carelessness. Such children cannot really be said to be careless, however, since their misfortunes arise from inborn aspects of temperament. Ways in which you can help impulsive children overcome some of their difficulties are explained later.

How reflective children respond

In many ways a reflective child is the mirror image of an impulsive youngster. They are careful, thoughtful and seldom speak without weighing their words carefully. This can give the impression of a certain lack of spontaneity and a rather over-cautious approach to life. The reflective child is good at forward planning and can anticipate the likely consequences of any action with a fair degree of accuracy. Their powers of selective attention are high, which makes them less prone to careless mistakes. They can concentrate for reasonably long periods without difficulty which helps them to classroom success. Their control usually extends to physical movements which means they are less accident-prone and better coordinated than the impulsive child.

How the average child responds

Children who gained an average score on this assessment display some of the characteristics of both reflective and impulsive children, but rarely show the extremes of behaviour found in either.

Their powers of concentration will be fairly good and they will be moderately careful and conscientious in their work. On occasions you may find them blurting things out unthinking, but at other times they will only speak or act after giving the matter thought. In many ways this is an ideal temperamental balance, since they avoid the pitfalls lying in wait for the over-impulsive child, yet show a more lively and spontaneous approach to life than is usually found in the highly reflective youngster.

Reflective and average children do not, generally, require much help since their temperaments are far better suited to the demands of life than the over-impulsive youngster. If your own child achieved an average score on the assessment, but sometimes gets into difficulties through impulsive behaviour, however, you will find the procedures described below of value.

Helping the impulsive child

As we have seen, one of the main difficulties confronting impulsive children is their tendency to speak and act without thinking. A second important failing is their inability to concentrate effectively or to focus attention firmly enough on the key aspects of a particular task.

Although the extent to which a child is impulsive (or reflective) is due to inborn characteristics of their nervous system, studies have shown that you can nevertheless reduce impulsivity by teaching the child different ways of thinking and responding. While you will never eliminate impulsive behaviour entirely nor, perhaps, should you attempt to do so, it is possible to help the child become more attentive and reflective in specific situations when learning anything new, for instance, or answering questions in class.

Research by Dr Bonnie Camp, Professor of Pediatrics and Psychiatry at the University of Colorado Medical School, and Mary Ann Bash of the University of Northern Colorado, has shown that one of the best ways to help impulsive children think more carefully and behave more cautiously is by getting them to develop a specific plan of action for each situation and then to work through it step by step. The *Thinking Aloud* programme, which they developed on the basis of their work with children, is now widely used and has proved extremely successful.

Here's how to use it to guide your own impulsive youngster. The child is taught to ask himself or herself four questions whenever confronted by the need to solve a problem, make a decision or deal with an unfamiliar situation.

What is the problem? *or* What should I do?

What plan should I use? *or* How can I do it?

Am I using my plan?

How did I do?

What is the problem – What should I do
The first question compels impulsive children to stop and think about what is expected of them. It also makes them rephrase

the question or instruction in their own words. This is important since it often happens that a child fails to come up with the expected response simply because the task was imperfectly understood.

What plan should I use – How can I do it

The second question is designed to draw the child's attention to the strategies they have been taught for dealing with that type of situation. The precise nature of this plan will, of course, vary according to the demands of the situation. Always check that the child really knows how to solve a particular problem, reach a decision or handle a social encounter. If there are failures in their understanding, or gaps in their knowledge, sort these out before helping them create an effective plan of action.

Am I using my plan?

The third question makes the impulsive child pause and think, while carrying out the plan, to check that what should be done really is being done. This is important because it helps avoid careless errors. Sometimes even though an impulsive child has an excellent plan for a particular task, he starts growing confused and gets lost before arriving at the desired result. Where the plan is a long one, the child should be instructed to ask this question at regular intervals during its execution.

How did I do?

Finally, with the answer found, the choice made or the activity completed, the child should be encouraged to review his performance. He should focus, not merely on any mistakes or misjudgments, but also on all the positive aspects of his or her approach. In this way motivation is sustained while allowing the plan to be modified so that any errors which arose can be avoided the next time that the plan is followed.

Teaching the procedure

Start by making sure your child fully understands each of the four questions. With young children you may find it helpful to suggest that they copy out and colour the pictures in illustrations 9–12, which show the steps to take. These can then be pasted on to card and displayed on the family noticeboard or in their room. Construction toys and jigsaw puzzles are useful practice materials for children aged 4–8. With older children you should provide help in structuring plans which deal with the practical problems they face at school.

Start by asking your child to define the problem. In the case of a jigsaw puzzle this would obviously be to join all the pieces together in the correct order. Ask your child to describe the task aloud, using his, or her, own words. Next develop a plan: with the jigsaw a logical first step is to find all the straight edges and fit the outer framework together first. Once again, have your child repeat this part of the plan in their own words. The next step could be to find the pieces which make up some of the larger parts of the picture. As before, your child should incorporate this instruction into their plan by going over it in their own words.

If there are any unexpected difficulties when the plan is first put into action, it can be modified to remove them. Each time changes are made, the child should talk through them aloud.

The jigsaw plan might sound something like this:
Child: 'I am going to fit all the pieces of this puzzle together.' (states the problem clearly)
'First I will sort out all the pieces with one or two straight sides. Next I will find the four corners.' (begins to work through his plan)
'I will join all the outside parts together.' (develops the plan)
'When the outside is finished, I will look for pieces which make up the big parts of the picture...'
The child continues to develop the plan in this way.

Impulsive children often have a low tolerance for frustration, and this should be allowed for. In the case history on which this example is based, seven-year-old Michael tended to throw his partly completed puzzle across the room in a fury whenever he became stuck. Michael was told to include in his plan a strategy for coping with these moments of frustration.

Child: 'When I start getting cross because the puzzle won't come out right, I must stop doing it and work at something else until I don't feel angry any more.'

ILLUSTRATION 9
What is the problem?

ILLUSTRATION 10
How can I do it?

ILLUSTRATION 11
Am I using the plan?

ILLUSTRATION 12
How did I do it?

Every so often the child is taught to pause and ask himself:
Child: 'What stage have I got to in my plan? How is the plan working out? What should I be doing next?'

With the puzzle complete the child reviews what has been achieved.
Child: 'How did I do? Did my plan work out OK, or should I make some changes next time I use it?'

At first the child should practise working through the plan by talking each stage out loud. When putting it into practice in school, or with other children, he will, of course, go through it silently.

The plan approach can be used for any situation. In class the impulsive child might be taught to use a plan along these lines:
'When I have made certain I understand the question, I will:
Think back over all the facts which I know about that topic.
Pick out the ones which are important in answering this question or solving this problem.
Put them together to make an answer.
Check my answer to make sure I have not overlooked any important points and that my facts are correct.
When writing it down, read the answer to make sure I have put down exactly what I wanted to say.
Move to the next problem.

Similar action plans can be devised for any situation, social or academic, in class or at home; but don't work out the plans for your child. It is far better if they are created with their active involvement, as in this discussion between a mother and her nine-year-old son Alex, whose habit of blurting out tactless, and often hurtful, remarks had lost him many friends.

Mother: What did you say to Ellen?
Alex: I said she was a fat cow and I hated her... I said everybody did.
Mother: Why did you say that... how do you think she felt?
Alex: Well, it's true. She is fat... anyhow I didn't really mean it. It was just a sort of joke.
Mother: Did it make her laugh?

Alex: She started to cry.

Mother: How about you? How did you feel?

Alex: Well, afterwards I felt bad. I didn't want to upset her. But she started it. She said something bad about me first.

Mother: Thinking about it, afterwards, what would you sooner have done?

Alex: Said something else... or not anything. Just kept quiet.

Mother: You quite often say things and then wish you hadn't, don't you?

Alex: Suppose so...

Mother: How could you stop yourself?

Alex: Well, I could bite my lip, or hold my breath. That would stop me.

Mother: Biting your lip sounds painful. Why not hold your breath, say, for the time it takes to count slowly to five.

Alex: OK, but suppose I want to say something else... not bad.

Mother: Well, you could think about that while holding your breath. You could use the time to think of something better to say.

Alex's plan, then, is quite simply to respond to any insulting or irritating remark by holding his breath, counting slowly up to five while thinking about – instead of blurting out – his answer. The boy now rehearses his plan a few times:

Mother: What are you supposed to do?

Alex: If somebody says something that upsets me, I am going to hold my breath, then count to five. I'm going to think out what I want to say and then say it.

Mother: What will you do if you feel like blurting something out?

Alex: I'll use my plan.

As you can see there is nothing especially difficult about this procedure and the child can easily learn a number of plans covering the main situations where impulsive behaviour causes difficulties.

While teaching this procedure be sure to allow the child ample thinking time after posing a particular question. For example, if you ask: 'What is your plan?', do not be tempted to rush in and supply the answer if a reply is not forthcoming almost immediately. One of the reasons why impulsive children blurt out their answers is that they feel under pressure from the adult. They have learned that unless a response is more or less immediate, the grown-up will rephrase and repeat the question or perhaps give them the solution. In either event they tend to feel humiliated or cheated – especially if, as so often happens, they knew the right answer. Do not be afraid therefore, to allow thinking time during which the child can pause, reflect and organize his or her thoughts before replying.

Finally, you can help the impulsive child overcome problems of attention by breaking down learning tasks into smaller and more manageable components. Even with adults, studies have shown that the ability to concentrate hard on any one topic is usually limited to around 20 minutes, after which the mind starts to wander. For impulsive children the span of attention may be five minutes or less. Instead of trying to force them to attend for much longer periods, organize any work being done at home so that it is broken up into periods of study lasting no more than ten minutes. After each session the child has a short break. In this way learning becomes less daunting.

The extent to which children's behaviour and ability is influenced by impulsivity-reflectivity is, as we have stressed, largely the result of inborn temperamental factors, and the impulsive child cannot therefore be blamed for his or her approach to life. With the easily mastered and effective thinking strategy described above, impulsive children can be taught to enjoy the benefits of rapid and spontaneous responses to events, without having to pay a heavy price in classroom failure and adult disapproval.

CHAPTER TEN

Assessing your child's creativity

Long before children have developed any real artistic technique, their pictures provide us with clues to their creativity. We make a highly subjective assessment of the imagination they reveal through such things as their use of colour, their sense of design, the sort of details included and the fluency with which fantasy is visualized on paper.

Like all subjective assessments, these judgments tend to be biased by our perceptions and prejudices. A painting that strikes one adult as revealing a highly creative child may be dismissed by another as a talentless daub. This often penalizes the highly creative child whose powers of imagination are so vivid that they are constantly trying to break free of conventional restraints to explore new ways of expressing their ideas and inspirations. This chapter tells you how you can avoid such pitfalls and reach a more objective understanding of a child's creative ability by means of drawings and paintings. The fact that this is possible has been shown by a number of major psychological studies around the world. In one, Professor Paul Torrance, of the University of California at Los Angeles, assessed the creativity of several hundred children when they first started secondary school. He did this by means of simple drawing exercises, similar to those that follow. Many years later he renewed contact with as many of the original group as he could find.

The results were intriguing. Among the high scorers on his assessment was a far higher percentage of men and women who, by their activities and achievements, clearly demonstrated a high level of creativity. These men and women wrote books, plays, and poetry. They painted, sculpted, and composed or played music. Several had established a reputation in some creative field, such as the theatre, cinema, photography, design, publishing or advertising. It was not only in the arts, however, that they showed above-average levels of creativity. They were also prominently represented among scientists carrying out original and creative research.

You may well find early signs of such talents in your own children, but this is not the real reason why you should make the assessment. It is equally important to identify, at as early an age as possible, those children whose creative potential is not being successfully developed. When this is done it is often possible to enhance their creativity by means of exercises disguised as enjoyable games. This is more important than some people realize since being able to think in original and unconventional ways is essential to success in a wide range of intellectual activities, in the sciences as well as the arts.

Assessing creativity

In this picture assessment you are going to be looking at two important aspects of creativity – fluency and originality. By fluency we mean the speed at which a child's imagination functions, that is the number of ideas he or she can dream up in a specific period of time. For this part of the test it is quantity rather than quality which matters. Clearly, however, simply coming up with a vast number of useless ideas is not helpful, so it is also necessary to assess the quality of those ideas by scoring them according to their originality.

To carry out the assessment, provide suitable drawing materials, including plenty of paper, and say something along these lines: 'This is a drawing game to see how many pictures you can make which have a circle or circles in them. These circles can be any size you like, but every drawing must have at least one of them. So draw the circle, or circles, first and then see how many different things you can turn them into. Keep on doing that until you run out of ideas and can't think of any more pictures to make with circles.' Children can take as long as they want over this task, but all the drawings should be completed in one session, and you can then score the pictures.

Fluency
To assess this simply count the number of separate drawings the child has completed. Only those based on at least one circle can be included.

Originality
The lists below contain examples of the type of pictures to include in each of the three scoring categories. It may well be that some of your child's drawings are not included, in which case you must assess their originality as follows. If the circle forms a major part of the drawing, which contains little else by way of embellishment or decorative details, place it in List 1. Where the circle, or circles, have provided the starting-point for drawing a more detailed picture, place it in List 2.
To qualify for List 3, the circle must form only a minor and fairly insignificant portion of the entire drawing.

Originality

List 1
Score 1 point for any of the following:

Plate	Wheel
Saucer	Coin
Ball	Hoop
Sun	Orange
Moon	Apple
etc, on its own.	

The drawings in illustrations 1a–c would be placed in List 1.

List 2
Score 2 points for any of the following:

Human
Animal
Any form of wheeled transport
Hat

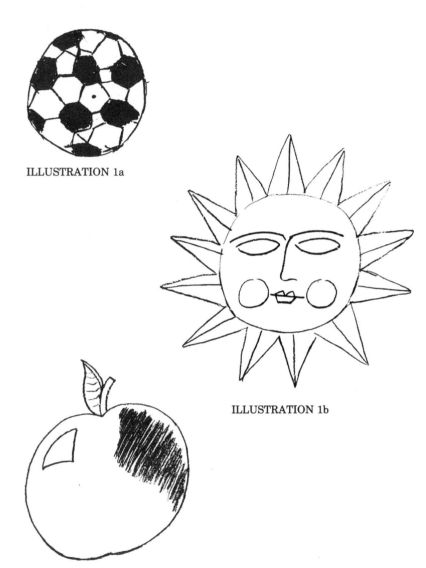

ILLUSTRATION 1a

ILLUSTRATION 1b

ILLUSTRATION 1c

Ashtray with cigarettes in it or standing on table
Archery or pistol shooting target
Pot or jar seen from above
Snowball
Barbells for weightlifting
Hole in the ground
Glasses – reading or sunglasses
Binoculars or telescope
Window in house
Stool
Pendulum
Shield with decoration
Cracker
Ornament(s) on Christmas tree
Lamp or light bulb
Insect
Clock or watch
Collection of fruit in container
Flying saucer or balloon

The drawings in illustration 2a–d would be placed in List 2.

List 3
Score 3 points for any of the following:

A door with the circle forming the knob
A ship with circles as portholes or the tops of funnels
Look-out on a vessel's mast
Ventilation pipes on ships
Propeller on ship or aircraft
Opening of a cave with a monster (or similar) emerging
Holes in piece of cheese
Manhole-cover in the street with a person climbing out
Aerial view of a circus ring or arena
A person juggling round objects (hoops, balls, etc)
Snowflakes
Circles forming part of a chain-of-office
An open mouth in a face
Person blowing bubbles from a pipe
A person holding a microphone

ILLUSTRATION 2a

ILLUSTRATION 2b

ILLUSTRATION 2c

bowl of fruit.

ILLUSTRATION 2d

ILLUSTRATION 3a

Sarah Ginns
age 10.

ILLUSTRATION 3b

ILLUSTRATION 3c

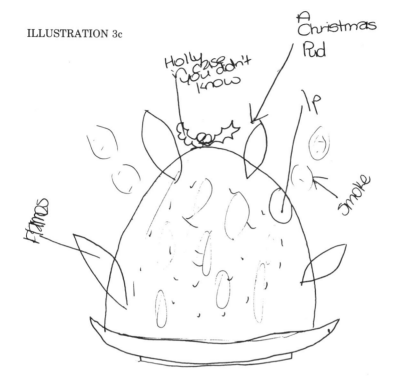

ILLUSTRATION 3d

The letter O in a word or the numeral O in a number
Helmet for a spaceman
Face of animal, or part of face.
Lens in camera, glasses or human eye
Discus thrower
Coin(s) as minor part of a larger drawing

The pictures in illustrations 3a–d would be included in List 3.

Now total the score and find out what your child's result means in terms of fluency and originality from the chart below.

Child's age	*Fluency*			*Originality*		
	Low	Medium	High	Low	Medium	High
4– 5	1– 3	4– 6	7+	1– 3	4– 8	8+
6– 7	1– 4	5– 8	9+	1– 6	7–12	12+
8– 9	1– 8	9–15	16+	1–12	13–28	28+
10–11	1–12	13–18	19+	1–24	24–35	35+
12–13	1–12	13–20	20+	1–30	30–45	45+

What your child's score tells you

Above-average fluency
Children with above-average fluency scores are often more extravert and happy-go-lucky than other children with a tendency to act impulsively and to be somewhat incautious. Their fluency is probably part of a generally inquisitive outlook on life. They are likely to ask a great many questions, have a strong desire to explore, and to discover and understand new things.

Originality
The higher the originality score, the greater the child's creative potential. The art of being creative is, after all, to see the world in a different way or to take an everyday situation and view it through fresh eyes. The link between intelligence and creativity, a mental skill sometimes called divergent thinking, has been investigated by Professor J C Guilford, who showed that while one can be intelligent without being creative, it is impossible to be creative without also being intelligent. The challenge facing parents and teachers, therefore, is to help the child harness this talent and channel his or her creativity into the most productive activities.

High fluency – low originality
Children with this pattern of scores are going for quantity instead of quality in their ideas. They tend to be lacking in true creativity and to be somewhat superficial in their approach to creative challenges. However, such youngsters are well on their way to being creative, and with your help can probably overcome their current inability to think more imaginatively.

High originality – low fluency
Although children who obtain this balance of scores are perfectly capable of producing highly original work, they need to take their time over it. This may mean that the child will succeed in and feel more attracted towards the kind of creative thinking demanded by scientific research rather than artistic occupations. This is especially true if the child scores high on the IQ assessments in chapter 11. Because scientific research usually takes place over a relatively long period there is more time to consider a variety of possible approaches and reflect on the best methods to adopt. By comparison, the creative demands placed on people in writing, advertising, publishing, the theatre and films and in design and painting are often made against urgent deadlines.

High fluency – high originality
This is clearly the best possible combination of scores and you should actively encourage your child in a wide range of creative pursuits. Your task is to make sure that the child is given plenty of scope to explore and expand his or her powers of imagination, not only by providing the raw materials for creativity – paints, paper, modelling materials, construction kits and so on – but also by creating an atmosphere in which creative thinking can flourish. While providing materials and opportunities for creativity, however, be careful not to try and direct your child too firmly along any particular pathway. Creative children are happiest and most successful when able to develop their own leisure activities, which can range from painting to computer programming and from model-making to writing poetry.

Low fluency – low originality
Children who scored low on both parts of the assessment are

likely to lack creativity. They may not show much curiosity about the world around them, asking few questions and generally accepting the ideas of others. It is also likely that they are more dependent than most, somewhat cautious and unwilling to act on their own initiative.

If your child comes into this category, it would be quite wrong, however, to conclude that he or she is any less intelligent than the high scorers. As we explained earlier, it is perfectly possible for clever children to fail on creatively demanding tasks, not because of any innate inability but simply because their imagination has not been sufficiently stimulated and enhanced.

Bright, non-creative children are sometimes described as 'convergent thinkers', which means they do best when tackling problems where there can only be one correct answer, the kind of challenge you find in arithmetic or when solving a crossword puzzle, for example. Convergent thinking is an extremely important skill in many areas of science and technology and should be valued. Since many of the subjects taught in school, and many of the problems posed in exams, are convergent in nature, children who are good at convergent tasks often do better than most in class.

It will, nevertheless, be helpful for such children's later success, and their complete development, if you can enhance their innate creativity. Even in technical and scientific subjects at which the convergent problem solver excels, there is often a need to bring creative thinking to bear on a particularly tricky or complex task. It frequently happens that the only way of producing the right answer is by approaching problems using the imagination, rather than logic alone.

Fortunately, creativity can be taught. The fact that a child shows little imagination does not mean that he or she was born without this talent. The potential for highly original thinking is present in every child and can be developed by providing the right kind of encouragement and guidance.

Medium fluency – medium creativity
This pattern of results, or any other combinations involving either *medium fluency* or *medium creativity* means that your child's fluency and/or freedom of imagination would benefit by

being more fully developed. There is, however, a good foundation on which to build and the enjoyable games described below will prove helpful in expanding his or her creativity.

The importance of creativity

Creative, or divergent, thinking is needed whenever you are given a problem for which there can be a number of equally valid answers. In the drawing test to assess creativity, for instance, some of the pictures displayed far more imagination than others, but all those constructed around circles were equally 'correct'.

Some children are better at solving convergent than divergent problems. An ability to use one's imagination effectively is now a crucial component of success in many careers not normally regarded as requiring much creative thought, such as mathematics, physics, chemistry, biology, engineering, computer programming, and electronics. Research in all these expanding fields demands men and women who can use their imagination – their divergent abilities – as well as convergent thinking skills.

With the exception of a few specialist subjects such as English, drama and art, modern education unfortunately offers little encouragement to children who are better at using their creative talents. In most science and technical subjects, students are penalized for not using approved answer-finding strategies. Exam success too, depends largely on being able to remember and recall established facts as quickly and as accurately as possible in order to produce the right answers to convergent-type questions. Since a student's reports, grades and final qualifications all depend so crucially on reasoning in the approved way, it is little wonder that children, teachers and parents are biased in favour of this type of thinking.

The danger in depending almost exclusively on convergent problem-solving procedures is that they can so narrow one's vision that it becomes impossible to see better ways of tackling the task. Your mind gets into a mental rut, a type of intellectual shortsightedness known as a 'set', which prevents the discovery of alternative methods. The phrase below is an example of just such a 'set' in action:

PARIS IN THE

THE SPRING

If you read that as PARIS IN THE SPRING look again. You were misled by seeing only what you expected to see.

In one of numerous experiments which explored this type of tunnel vision, subjects were given a matchbox, candle and drawing-pin, and then asked how they might fix the candle to the wall of a room using only the materials provided. The solution was to empty the matchbox and use the tray as a candle holder, having fastened it to the wall with the drawing-pin. When the box was supplied closed, filled with matches, the answer was found by far fewer subjects than if the box was provided empty and open, with the matches alongside. The reason was that the people were blinded to a second, equally valid, use for the box because they were seeing it solely as a container for matches. If that sounds obvious, see whether you can come up with answers to the two questions below, both of which demand divergent thinking if you are going to get them right.

Problem one
Copy illustration 4 on to a sheet of paper and complete it by writing the appropriate letters inside and outside the circle.

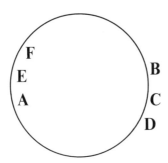

ILLUSTRATION 4

Problem two

Construct four triangles out of just six matches. None of the matches can be broken or used more than once.

If you managed to solve both easily and quickly it suggests you have a fairly strong talent for divergent thinking. If you found them hard, don't worry: you can still help your child enhance his or her creativity, and improve your own divergent skills at the same time. (Answers to the problems can be found at the end of this chapter.)

Teaching your child creative thinking

Here are three excellent drawing games which will help children develop their natural powers of creative thought. When playing them, keep each session fairly short to sustain motivation, and avoid competition between children as this will prove humiliating for the less imaginative child and may inhibit his or her development. The atmosphere should always be relaxed and good-humoured.

Crazy inventions

First think up some highly unlikely problem and then ask your child to create an equally crazy invention to provide the answer. A few ideas to get you started are given below. Encourage way-out answers – the sort of mad machines designed by the humourist W Heath Robinson give a good idea of what is needed.

Allow your child's sense of fantasy to run free: remember that you are not looking for the most practical solution but for the most interesting and unusual. Never say: 'That's stupid...' or 'How on earth could you do that...?', since such comments only make the child anxious and inhibited. It is very often exactly this mixture of anxiety and inhibition which has been hampering creativity in the past.

Starting ideas

A sailor is stranded on a desert island. You can imagine that he has salvaged almost anything you like from the shipwreck, except a boat or a radio. Draw a picture showing how he might:

Send a message

Escape by sea or air

Fight off an attack by pirates

Trap a dangerous monster as big as a building

Construct a vehicle to travel over the island, one that can cope with swamps and jungles

Somebody has dropped a valuable necklace into a deep lake. Draw a crazy-looking machine for locating and recovering the jewels.

Jimmy has a lot of trouble getting up in the morning. Invent something to get him out of bed, wash and dress him in time for school.

A dentist wants to be able to pull out teeth while watching television in another room. Devise an invention, built out of objects you might find around the house or shed, which would allow him to do so.

When children have played this game a few times, get them to start dreaming up their own improbable problems before drawing equally unlikely solutions to them.

Draw a shape

This game is similar to the creativity test, only instead of starting off with a circle or circles, the child begins with some other kind of geometric shape, such as a triangle, oblong or polygon. You can save time by having a series of cardboard shapes made to provide a template for these shapes.

You can, if you wish, assess these pictures for fluency and originality using the same method as before. By getting your child to play this game at regular intervals it becomes possible to monitor their creative development.

Draw a story

Unlike the first two games this involves both drawing and storytelling, which help to improve the child's visual and verbal imagination. Start by asking the child, or a group of children, to draw pictures on 15–20 cards – postcards are ideal for this purpose. Each drawing should be of just one thing, an animal, building, person or object. They can then be coloured for added effect.

The picture cards are shuffled and then the top one placed face up on the table. Whoever is starting – and for the first few games this had better be you – invents a story based on the picture. They have to go on talking for a certain amount of time – 20–30 seconds is usually long enough. A second card is turned up and the next player has to continue with the story, introducing the new picture. At the end of their turn a third card is is turned over and the next player takes up the tale. In this way a host of different stories can be created which challenge the child's powers of imagination.

Finding a use

The idea is to take some familiar household object – such as a cup, knife, paper-clip, safety-pin, spool of cotton or fountain-pen – and draw unusual and original uses for it. This game, too, can be scored for fluency and originality.

When the object is a paper-clip, improbable uses would include: to pick a lock, to clean dust out of a carving, as a fish hook, to fasten braces to trousers if your buttons came off, several strung together as a necklace, magnetized and used as a compass needle, to make a fence in a model railway layout, as a switch to complete an electrical circuit using battery and bulb, with a droplet of water to form a magnifying glass.

The object of the game is to help the child break away from the prison imposed by 'set' and to start viewing the familiar in a new and original manner.

As well as these games, you can enhance your child's natural creative ability by following these simple guidelines:

Provide plenty of opportunities to experiment and to explore without too much adult guidance. Learning as well as creativity are improved when children discover answers for themselves. It is far more helpful to make available the means by which a solution can be found than to offer the answer itself.

Provide toys and games which allow scope for the imagination. A painting-by-numbers game offers nothing more than a foregone conclusion. Paints and paper alone offer limitless scope for the imagination.

Avoid comments which cause the child to associate being creative with being criticized. Even if you do not think much of an idea, avoid saying so bluntly. Instead, use the child's proposals as the basis for exploring different ideas. See if you can help him or her find ways of improving on the original concept so that it becomes a more practical proposition.

Adopt the same approach when the child offers fantastic explanations about why things happen: for instance, claiming that tides happen because, twice a day, a giant steps into the sea to take a bath, or saying that a volcanic eruption is produced by a bad-tempered dragon breathing fire. If you are primarily a convergent thinker who prefers answers to be factually accurate, then this habit may prove irritating – but try to see its value.

Children must, of course, learn scientific explanations for natural events and acquire the ability to think logically about life, but these skills do not have to be gained at the loss of the young child's naturally vivid, and often fantastic, imagination.

Answers to problems one and two

1 Letters with straight lines and angles go inside the circle; letters with curves in their shapes go outside. The trick here is to see the alphabet not as symbols but as geometric designs.
2 The only way to form four triangles from six matches is to create a three-dimensional pyramid. Divergent thinking takes you away from attempts to form the triangle in only two dimensions.

CHAPTER ELEVEN

How pictures reveal intelligence

There can be few areas of psychological assessment so surrounded by controversy or fraught with risks as the objective testing of intelligence. Until recently, many psychologists, parents and teachers believed that it was possible to measure a child's IQ, Intelligence Quotient, by using a variety of paper and pencil tests. On the basis of their results, youngsters have been streamed into categories of cleverness according to that all-powerful IQ number. Those identified by the assessment as the brightest and the best were given opportunities for advancement denied the majority.

Those who devised and set these tests believed that intelligence was no mere abstract concept, a useful term to describe a varied selection of mental abilities, but something almost tangible within the brain which could be measured with the same precision as the child's height or weight. Like height and weight, it was also regarded by many as the result of inborn factors which neither child nor parent could hope to control. Just as tall parents are more likely to give birth to children of above-average height so, it was argued, will bright men and women have a greater chance of producing clever offspring. Seen from this viewpoint, therefore, one's intelligence became more or less a matter of genetic roulette. Having been created either bright or dull from the earliest moments of life you were then condemned to stay that way for life.

The dangers of classifying children according to their supposed abilities and attributes were described in the first chapter, where we warned of the powerful influence of the self-fulfilling prophecy. Nowhere, however, is this hazard more acute than in the area of intelligence testing. There is now ample research evidence to support the belief, held by sensible parents and perceptive teachers for decades, that by tying a 'clever' or 'stupid' tag around a child's neck we make it far more likely that he or she will turn out as predicted. You will probably recall the chilling story of the New York nursery school with its three tables for the achieving children, the average children and the inadequate children.

Intelligence is neither an inborn mental attribute nor a fixed and unchanging intellectual skill, and, indeed, as one of the authors has demonstrated, intelligence can be taught. (See *You Can Teach Your Child Intelligence* by David Lewis, Souvenir Press, London.) The assessment of intellectual development through drawing tests is described here for two reasons. Firstly, even in the absence of formal assessments, children are still ranked according to their assumed levels of intelligence. Go into any home or classroom in the country and you will soon be informed which youngsters are clever, which are average and which are stupid. Such judgments arise in a number of ways. The child's schoolwork, end-of-term reports, marks, grades and examination results offer a major source of 'enlightenment'. Students who score high marks are generally seen as more intelligent than those who do badly.

Without knowledge of their school results to guide us, we may assess a child intuitively on how brightly they shine during our chats with them. Do they ask clever questions? Do they learn quickly? Do they understand the answers they are given? Do they look and sound mentally alert? It is true that all the rule-of-thumb tests we have described can help pick out intelligent children. Those who acquire new skills rapidly, ask interesting questions, show a lively curiosity about the world and get good marks in class are certainly using their brains efficiently.

The opposite conclusion, that children who do none of these things are unintelligent, can be deeply misleading. As we have seen there are many aspects of personality, emotion and temperament which can undermine a child's intellectual performance:

The impulsive child who lacks the ability to concentrate and is careless when answering questions

The over-anxious child who feels too stressed to pay attention in class or to think clearly during exams

The low energy focus youngster who finds it difficult to invest sufficient effort in his studies

None of these children is necessarily any less intelligent than the academic high-flyers. The trouble is, of course, that they are labelled as 'dull' or 'mediocre', perhaps quite early on in their school careers, and so come to see themselves – and to be regarded by parents and teachers – as much less bright than other children.

The purpose of arriving at some more objective insight into their intellectual abilities now becomes clear. Suppose your child is not doing especially well in class, and you have assumed that this is because he or she is not especially clever. After carrying out the assessment we describe below, you will discover that this assumption is wrong. Your child is, it appears, far more intellectually capable than current attainments seem to suggest. You can now question why classroom achievement does not reflect this level of ability.

It may well be that some of the assessments you have already carried out have provided the answers you seek. With your deeper, and rather more accurate, understanding of your child's personality, emotions and temperament, some of the barriers to success may have become apparent already. It should then be possible to start working towards their final and complete removal using the practical procedures described.

Assessing intelligence through drawings

If you have any firsthand experience of IQ tests, it may come as something of a surprise to learn that you can make a reliable assessment of a child's intellectual development through his or her drawings. Most intelligence tests, it is true, ask questions and expect answers which are either right or wrong. The child might, for example, have to complete a number series, like this:

2 3 5 8 ? 21

Or find the odd one out:

Apple   Pear   Orange   Potato

The closest most IQ test get to drawings is in their use of geometric designs. The child either has to complete a series by selecting the identifying design from a number of alternatives, or has to say which one of a set of designs does not belong. In neither case, however, is the child actually asked to draw anything. Children's pictures were used effectively, however, to assess intelligence long before the first IQ test was invented.

Nearly a century ago the Italian educationalist, Professor Corrado Ricci, published convincing research evidence which clearly established a relationship between certain features in children's drawings and their level of intellectual development. Although Ricci urged teachers to adopt his method, they received little serious attention. More than twenty years were to pass before the French psychologist Alfred Binet developed the first paper and pencil IQ test at the request of his government. Binet's admirable intention was to provide the means for identifying children with learning difficulties in order to give them additional help. At that time, and for several years afterwards, there was no intention of using the tests for the purposes of classification and segregation. Alfred Binet's assessment method, which offered no scope for a child's drawing skills, set the pattern for the many hundreds that were to follow. Although neglected by teachers and educationalists, Ricci's work nevertheless aroused considerable interest among research psychologists.

In the last hundred years the value of drawings in the assessment of intelligence has been widely investigated both in the United States and in Europe. Hundreds of learned articles and a small mountain of statistics now bear testimony to the powerful relationship between features in a child's pictures and important aspects of intellect. So well do drawings reflect intellectual potential that researchers have discovered it is possible to make a valid assessment from nothing more complicated than two lines drawn on a sheet of plain paper.

This remarkable finding was made a few years ago by Drs Amia Lieblich, Anat Ninio, and Sol Kugelmass, at the University of Jerusalem. As part of their investigation of child development, these three psychologists examined the direction in which children, aged four to six, drew vertical and horizontal lines.

If you have a child in this age group, you may be interested to repeat their experiment in order to gain an approximate measure of your child's mental development. Out of sight of the child draw two straight lines with a ruler, exactly six inches long. One should be perfectly vertical, the other perfectly horizontal. Now show these to your child and ask him to draw them on a sheet of A4 sized paper. A ruler can be used if he or she wishes. As this is being done, watch carefully and note whether the horizontal line is drawn from right to left or left to right across the page and whether the vertical line is drawn downwards from the top of the paper or upwards from the bottom of the paper.

When they made this simple test, the Israeli investigators found that those drawing the horizontal line from left to right and the vertical line from top to bottom were likely to possess higher than average levels of intelligence for their age. The researchers explained their result as follows: when very young children spontaneously choose to draw straight lines from left to right, their preference is probably a reflection of the left-to-right direction of handwriting when using Western scripts. Here not only the lines themselves, but also horizontal strokes in letters, are formed by a movement towards the right of the paper. They suggest that a greater familiarity with left-right lines, below the age of six, indicates an understanding of writing skills which is, in turn, a function of mental development. The same explanation is offered for top-to-bottom choice on the vertical line, since the ascending and descending strokes of printed letters – the style used by children learning to write – are also formed in this direction.

This test is offered more as an interesting sidelight on the assessment of intelligence in very young children than as a procedure you should take too seriously. The following method, however, can assess intellectual ability with considerable accuracy.

Assessment of your child's intellectual development

During the years in which pictures have been used to assess
the intelligence of children, many different items have formed
their subject matter. The problem has been to find something
which is familiar to children over a wide age range and from
differing social and cultural backgrounds. This is no easy task
since even a child's concept of something as seemingly universal as the human figure varies from one country to another,
especially as regards hairstyle, clothes and skin colour. To
overcome this difficulty, Dr T R Sharma of the Punjabi
University in Patiala, India, has developed a test of mental
development based on the bicycle. He realized that, unlike
most complex artifacts, the humble bicycle undergoes little or
no significant changes from one part of the world to another. It
is familiar to children across a wide age range and from all
social classes.

The assessment we describe, developed by us from Dr
Sharma's original research, also uses a bicycle, but it is in no
way a test of your child's drawing ability. The absence or
presence of certain details, which provide the significant signs
in this test, are unrelated to artistic skills.

Carrying out the assessment

Give your child a sheet of white, unlined paper and ask for a
drawing of a bicycle. Explain that this should be an ordinary
bicycle, the sort children ride to school, not a specially designed
stunt or racing bicycle. Say you want it drawn very carefully
and in as much detail as possible. The picture can be in pencil,
fibre pen or ballpoint pen. There is no time limit, but the
drawing should be completed within one session.

Scoring the drawing

Look at the first feature described on the scoring scale below,
and then examine your child's drawing to see if this particular
item is included. If it is award the picture 1 point; for example,
a picture which included both wheels, would earn one mark. If
those wheels had spokes it would be worth a further point,
while a double set of crossing spokes gains a third point for the

drawing. Study their version of the bicycle carefully to make certain you do not overlook any of the features listed.

Feature	*Description*
Both wheels drawn	Can be circular or oval, but should be more or less the same size
Spokes	These count provided they point towards the middle of the wheel. Horizontal, parallel spokes do not count
Double-spokes	On either wheel. Double set crossing and touching the two ends of the hub
Valve	Any indication of a point where the tyres can be inflated. On either wheel
Mudguards	Must be shown on both wheels. Any sort of semicircular representation. Must be above the wheel.
Hubs	On either wheel, but has to be represented by a small circle, a point does not count
Tyres	On both wheels. Any indication of the tyre counts
Tread	Any representation of tread on the tyres
Central axle	Approximately in the centre of the bicycle, where the pedals go
Central wheel	To which pedals are attached
Teeth on central wheel	For turning the chain
Central wheel of correct size	Should not be greater than ¼ diameter of the cycle's wheels. No point awarded if it is larger than ⅓ the size of main wheels
Chain present	Should connect central wheel to rear hub. Must run on only one side of the

	bike. If full chainguard has been drawn, count this as also indicating a chain and give the point
Chain-links drawn	These can be represented as dotted lines or by small circles or ovals or by any means which shows the child's attempt to indicate the links
Pedals	Skill of drawing quite unimportant, only the idea which matters
Pedal connecting rods	Bars or rods, can be shown by a single or a double line
Inner pedal bars	On either pedal, the side and central bars shown in some way
Pedal rubbers	Should be drawn so as to distinguish them from the central metal bar
Free-wheel	Any indication of concept counts
Free-wheel teeth	To support chain. Can be shown in any way
Free-wheel the correct size	Should be about half the size of the central wheel. No point awarded if it is larger than $1/3$ of the central wheel.
Frame joining handle to saddle	Can be either straight (man's bike) or curved (lady's bike)
Frame joining handle to central axle	
Frame attaching saddle to central axle	
Frame joining saddle to rear-wheel	
Handles present	Arms bent at right angles, with a straight line emerging at right angles from the centre

Frame connecting handle-bars to front wheel	
Lamp clip	This counts for a point if a lamp or dynamo are shown, even if it is not specifically drawn in
Brakes with handle	Only count if shown on both sides
Saddle	
Saddle springs or rods	
Carrier	Should be drawn in lower than the saddle over the rear wheel
Stand	Any type
Stand shown in two dimensions	Also counts for a point if springs are shown or the stand is attached to the hub
Lamp or dynamo	
Red lamp on rear mudguard	
Basket	Can either be on the handles or above carrier
Bell	On either or both sides of handles
Pump	May be on the bike or shown separately
Mud flap(s)	

This makes a possible total of 40 points. The examples below should help make this scoring system clear.

The cycle in illustration 1, drawn by a 12-year-old, includes 11 of the features listed above.

Illustration 2, drawn by a 10-year-old, contains 23 of the key features.

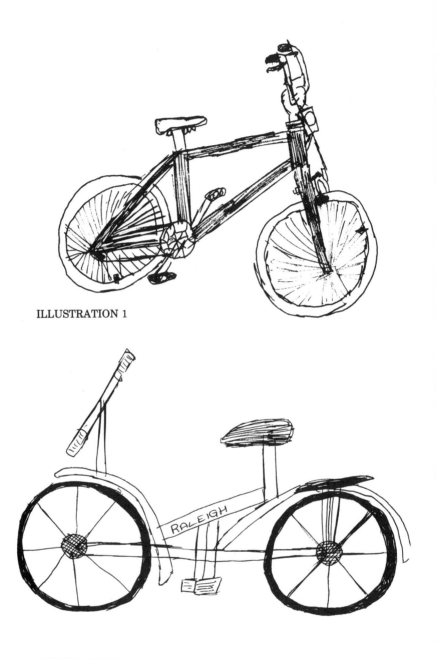

ILLUSTRATION 1

ILLUSTRATION 2

ILLUSTRATION 3

There are 36 of the listed items in illustration 3, drawn by a 14-year-old.

After checking your child's drawing for all the significant features and awarding a point for each one, total the score and use the rating chart to discover what the result reveals about your child's level of intellectual development.

Rating Scale

Age	Low	Average	High	Very High
4 – 5	0 – 2	3 – 7	8 – 14	15+
6 – 7	3 – 5	6 – 10	11 – 18	19+
8 – 9	5 – 7	8 – 12	13 – 20	21+
10 – 11	7 – 10	11 – 20	21 – 30	31+
12 – 14	10 – 15	16 – 25	26 – 35	35+

If your child achieved a high or very high score on this test it is reasonable to assume that he or she has well-developed intellectual abilities. Where current school performance is failing to reflect this level of intelligence consider whether personality or emotional factors are holding the child back.

There is no need to feel upset if your child's score has placed him in the average or low category: the result does not mean the youngster cannot hope to shine intellectually. As we explained earlier, intelligence is not a single, inborn mental ability but a series of interrelated thinking skills, all of which can be taught. All children have a tremendous potential for intellectual attainment which can be realized so long as the right lessons are given early enough.

Although providing a detailed training schedule is outside the scope of this book, here are some general pointers for helping children develop their brains more effectively:

Provide such children with every opportunity for exercising their minds for, like physical strength and stamina, mental power increases the more it is used and the harder the brain is made to work.

Try to encourage games which develop problem-solving skills. Word or number puzzles, constructional toys, electronic kits and chemistry sets are just a few of the practical pursuits which help to expand children's thinking skills.

Encourage the child's curiosity by responding in a positive way to their questions – however tedious or trivial some of these may seem. The essential thing is to get them into the habit of asking about anything and everything they do not understand. Many children become anxious and inhibited about putting questions to adults because they fear criticism or rejection. This means that simple misunderstandings may go unresolved and basic information is not acquired.

A positive response does not, however, mean that you should spoon-feed the child with facts and figures. Encourage the habit of looking up anything which is not understood. If you do not know the answer to a question do not be afraid to say so. Share the task of searching for the necessary information.

Give children as much freedom as possible to explore their surroundings and learn from their mistakes. Clearly the very young must be protected from dangers, but try not to curtail their independence any more than necessary.

Try to identify any anxieties associated with school or learning tasks which could be hampering the child's intellectual development. It quite often happens that children who have an average or below average score on this assessment are being held back by a fear of failing, one of the fears of childhood described in Chapter 12.

Revealing the fears of childhood

Maureen had been analysing the pictures of her ten-year-old son, Michael, for more than a year and finding the procedures very helpful in understanding the changing moods of a sometimes emotionally fraught little boy. Because Joanna, her five-year-old daughter, was so much more outgoing and communicative, Maureen had seen no reason for making similar assessments of her drawings and paintings. But, within a few weeks after starting school for the first time, Joanna became increasingly withdrawn and tearful. When asked why she was so unhappy, the girl said: 'I hate school...' but could not be persuaded to go into more detail.

Maureen was confident that picture analysis could help explore these feelings, but she then ran into a problem. While Michael enjoyed painting or drawing, and willingly took part in the assessment games, Joanna refused to cooperate. She would not draw more than scribbles and her few paintings were splashes of colour which conveyed little information. 'Jo really looked forward to going to school,' Maureen told us, 'and really seemed to be enjoying herself at first. Now she cries and clings to me when she gets there. She doesn't want to go into class and, after lessons, looks exhausted and miserable. Yet I can't get her to talk about it, or draw me pictures related to her school activities. So what do I do now?'

The answer was very simple. Maureen would make the drawings and Joanna would carry out the analysis. After just one session, it became clear that a major part of the girl's fears were being caused by an unpleasant teacher who appeared to have taken a dislike to her. Another problem was that, being a bright child, Joanna had been placed in a class of slightly older children. Although she could keep up with them intellectually, getting along socially was far more difficult. After a discussion with the head mistress, Joanna was moved to a different class and, before long, her fears about going to school had disappeared.

There may well be occasions when you will find the same approach helpful for identifying similar fears and conflicts in your own child. It is especially useful with children who are reluctant to paint or draw, and on those occasions when you want to make a more rapid assessment of their feelings about some major event. This might be starting a new school, going into hospital, or after an emotional crisis in the family such as a bereavement. You are concerned to discover exactly how the child is reacting and to identify any fears which have been aroused, but find him or her either unwilling or unable to disclose his or her innermost thoughts. In these circumstances you may well find the following procedure, which we have developed from the work of Dr Kenneth Appel, of the Pennsylvania Hospital Institute for Mental Hygiene, particularly helpful.

Making the drawings
You prepare for the analysis by producing two types of picture. The first consists of six abstract designs drawn on 12.5 × 17.5 cm (5 × 7in) cards (see illustration 1). You can either copy these directly or use them as the basis for creating similar pictures of your own. The great thing is to keep them simple and abstract.

You should now draw a series of pictures showing different aspects of the child's life, including all those situations you suspect may lie at the root of the problem. The pictures should be drawn on plain paper, approximately 10 × 8 in, and you should leave large margins in which notes can be written. You might include drawings of the school, the playground or your own home, for example. Do not include any figures because your child can sketch these in – stick-men are perfectly adequate – as you explore the scenes together. There

ILLUSTRATION 1

is no need to do especially detailed pictures, nor need you worry if they do not rate as great art. All that matters is that your child can both identify the scene and identify with the images. You are now ready to start the assessment session.

Your child makes the analysis

Sit comfortably side by side, and explain that you are going to play a new kind of game together. You have drawn some pictures and you want the child to make up stories about them, and you are going to make some notes, so that you do not forget what he or she has said.

Present the first of the abstract designs. Ask the child to guess what it shows. If he or she gets stuck, offer suggestions. Keep the game relaxed and good-humoured. Emphasize co-operation and enjoyment. Do not let the child think that you are carrying out some kind of test and that there are right or wrong answers. Keep the session flowing briskly along, but make a brief note – on a separate scrap of paper – as the child comes up with ideas about each of the designs in turn. Ask questions designed to help the child think carefully about each of the designs.

Which do you like best?

Which of the objects the designs remind you of do you prefer?

Why do you prefer that design?

There is no need to take up too much time on this part of the assessment, nor need you keep a detailed record of the child's answers. Although you can often gain some fascinating insights into your child's thinking at this stage, its main purpose is not to obtain information so much as to get children familiar with the task of talking about pictures and having their comments written down. When all the cards have been examined, select one of the larger drawings you have made and ask your child to look at it carefully. Then start asking questions and writing down the responses, in brief notes, around the margins of the picture.

Experience has shown that when the child's remarks are

jotted down openly and with enthusiasm this note-taking, far from inhibiting the flow of ideas, seems to stimulate comment and interest. The significance of writing down the ideas around the picture, rather than on a separate sheet of paper, is that they then become part of the image, a decorative embellishment which helps to focus the child's attention more powerfully on his or her feelings about the scene depicted.

Your questions will, of course, depend on the picture being analysed and the problems being explored. If it showed a school, and you were trying to discover the cause of your child's fears in the classroom, you might ask:

Whereabouts is your desk?

Who do you sit next to?

Who teaches you in that room?

Which part of the school do you like best?

What happens there? Who else is there?

Which teacher/other child do you like best?

Which teacher/other child do you like least?

Is there anybody there who makes you afraid?

Where do you go during the break?

What do you do before school starts?

Your child can answer these questions verbally and/or by pointing to the appropriate parts of the drawing. A better method, however, is to provide a pencil or pen and ask him to sketch in a small figure representing himself, or anybody else you are talking about. If the child protests that your drawing does not look like the school or house, etc., then offer to redraw it to the child's instructions and ask about the details you should include.

The success of this assessment depends on your maintaining the right atmosphere throughout. It is essential to display humour and interest while taking care to avoid any signs of irritation, criticism or censure, even if your child admits to wrongdoing. You must continue in the role of a fellow player in an entertaining game, rather than a grown-up sitting in judgment on what is being said. If this mood is sustained, you should find that even shy and reticent children who normally find self-disclosure difficult will become remarkably forthcoming, and willingly talk at length about their feelings and their fears.

Let's look at part of the conversation between Maureen and Joanna, as this provides a useful illustration of the kind of dialogue that occurs during a typical analysis session. It starts with Maureen showing her daughter the first of six abstract designs she has drawn and asking:

Maureen: What does that look like, Jo?

Joanna: Looks like a somebody asleep in bed.

Maureen: OK, how about this one?

Joanna: That's like ... looks like a cat with kittens.

Maureen: What are they doing?

Joanna: The Mummy cat is taking care of them. She's given them supper and now she's going to put them to bed.

Joanna goes on to identify other designs as showing a house with a big wall around it; a little girl being chased by an ugly giant; a Christmas tree and a castle where bad people live. Even at this stage some of the little girl's fantasies are starting to emerge as her imagination is stimulated. She has lost an initial reluctance to join in and now answers enthusiastically. After working through all her remaining cards, Maureen asks Joanna to pick the ones she likes best:

Joanna: I like the kittens best, then the house with the big wall, then the one with somebody in bed.

Maureen: How about the castle?

Joanna: No, that's creepy. That's where the giants live and they eat up people.

Maureen: Is that one of the giants chasing the little girl?

Joanna: Yes, and if he catches her she'll be eaten too.

Maureen: But if she gets to the house with the big wall she'll be safe. . .

Joanna: Yes, and then her Mummy will put her into bed and she won't get eaten by that old giant.

Maureen then moves on and shows Joanna her drawing of the school.

Joanna: That's where I go to school.

Maureen: That's right. Where is your classroom?

Joanna points to it.

Joanna: And that's where Miss Jessop takes off her coat and hat.

Maureen: Where do you sit in the room? Show me. . .

Joanna is given a pencil and draws in a little figure by one of the windows. She is then asked who sits next to her, who occupies the seat in front, whether she likes that seat or would sooner sit somewhere else, and so on. After exploring her daughter's feelings about the classroom, they move out into the playground and, once again, she asks Joanna to draw stick people to represent herself, her friends and the teacher.

Joanna: That's Miss Jessop, she takes break.

Maureen notices that the teacher is very much taller than the children and seems to loom menacingly over them. She asks her daughter to tell her what is going on.

Joanna: Well, Miss Jessop is telling us off because of the noise.

Maureen: Does she often tell you off?

Joanna: She gets very cross with us. . .

Maureen: Everybody? Does she get cross with all of you?

Joanna: Not with all of us. But she gets cross with me...

Maureen: Let's go back inside the classroom. Who sits next to you...?

In this short session, Maureen has been able to identify at least one possible cause of her daughter's distress. Later she adds to her knowledge by returning to the school drawing and exploring other activities in which Joanna may feel threatened by the teacher and overawed by her companions.

Drawing a dream

When you are uncertain exactly what sort of activities, or situations, may be making the child fearful – or on those occasions when they remain unforthcoming during an analysis of your own pictures – you may find it helpful to move from reality to fantasy and investigate the world of their dreams. If you feel that playing with the abstract design cards helps to break the ice and gets your child used to the idea of talking aloud about pictures, then start as described above. You can then introduce the dream drawing game by saying something along these lines:

Parent: I had a really strange dream last night. I am going to tell you all about it, and I want you to draw me a picture showing what happened.

You can then either recount a genuine dream or invent some suitable scene for the child to draw. If you have an idea of the things which have been troubling him or her, try to work these images into the dream; for example, one mother whose seven-year-old son was afraid of going to parties, described a dream in which she had been invited to a very lavish party in a big house. She explained in detail how the room was furnished and the guests were dressed, what they had to eat and drink and what games they played. 'After tea some of the people hid and the rest had to find them.' The boy, who had drawn the house, tea-table and guests, now began to 'hide' stick-men in different rooms. At this point, his mother noticed one figure hidden in a cupboard, but the door was deliberately shown open. She remarked jokingly that it would be easy to find him unless the door was closed. 'No, that would be too scary... he would die if you did that,' her son replied seriously. That gave her an idea, explored further during later drawing sessions, that he might be fearful of confined spaces.

She not only found that he was claustrophobic, but that he had been obliged to play hide-and-seek at a number of recent parties. When you have finished describing your own dream, ask the child to recount one of theirs which you then draw. This provides another excellent opportunity for investigating, through fantasy and wish-fulfilment, the child's conflicts and confusions. With the drawing completed, ask questions similar to those listed above and write down the information on the margins of the pictures.

By using these two approaches whenever children seem to be reacting fearfully to some situation, person or event, it becomes possible not only to get to the root of their difficulties but also to free communications between you. In many families, even warm and affectionate ones, such conversations are often all too rare. Without a frank and honest exchange of information about hopes and fears, dreams and disappointments there can be little real understanding or appreciation for another's feelings.

How children's drawings change

So far we have looked at changes in children's pictures caused by factors in their personality, by emotional states, aspects of temperament, feelings for others, creative ability and intellectual development. Many other, equally profound, changes also occur in their drawing and painting merely as a result of development influences. We have described how missing arms and hands, for example, reflect anxiety or dislike. While this can be a perfectly valid interpretation, one must also consider the fact that limbs are quite often missing from the drawings of very young children for quite different reasons. At the age of four, for example, arms are only included in around 45 per cent of children's drawings. By the age of six, this proportion has risen to 71 per cent, but even as late as twelve, about 5 per cent of children continue to omit arms from the human figures. In the latter case the almost total absence of arms is related to aspects of the child's physical and mental development, rather than emotions or feelings.

To understand the nature of these developmental changes, we should look briefly over the child's growing artistic skills. As part of our research, we have been following the picture-making talents of a group of children over a seven-year period. The illustrations below were produced by just one of them, Tracey. In her gradual progress from formless scribbles to formal drawings can be seen a typical pattern of knowledge and skill.

Scribbles

At 14 months, Tracey discovers the delights of scribbling (see illustration 2). The Danish psychologist Dr Helga Eng has aptly described these first shapeless, purposeless lines as: 'the primitive cell from which all graphic art grows'.

A child's scribbles are initially almost always wavy – like those shown above – because little muscle control is needed to make this kind of design. With sweeping movements of the arm, from elbow or shoulder, the child can produce a tangled

ILLUSTRATION 2

mess of lines totally lacking in any plan or expression. They tell us nothing about the infant's imagination and are not produced with any definite purpose in view; these wavy scribbles reflect the child's slowly evolving concept of movement. These marks on paper can be compared with the haphazard tracings of a pen attached to the bobbin of a gyrating pendulum. Gradually, however, wavy scribbles are interspersed with circular movements (see illustration 3). Although these scribbles, produced by Tracey at the age of 18 months, may appear equally formless and lacking in plan, they reveal that important basic lessons about drawing are nonetheless being mastered. These fundamental skills are the essential foundations on which formal drawing ability depends.

The initial impulse to scribble, which may have been the result of a chance experiment with a crayon on some easily marked surface or through watching another child drawing, is slowly brought under control of mind and body. Unlike wavy scribbles, circular ones require a degree of control over the muscles of hand, wrist and arm. They are the product not of

ILLUSTRATION 3

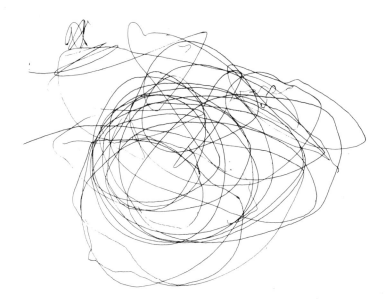

ILLUSTRATION 4

thoughtless movements but of a considered and carefully orchestrated collaboration between mind and body.

At the age of two, Tracey starts producing scribbles which include even more demanding lines, angles, zigzags and crosses (see illustration 4). This type of drawing requires considerable precision in the use of arm, wrist and finger muscles, while presenting a far greater challenge to the brain in terms of perception, memory and the coordination of hand

and eye movement. With each drawing of this type, Tracey is building up a store of knowledge about the way different motions of the crayon produce varying results on the paper. This information will be used with increasing frequency as the child moves from the formless scribble to a more accurate and realistic representation of her world. In some children this type of scribble continues alongside a gradually increasing skill in making more formal, recognizable pictures.

As Tracey's attachment to lines and angles grows there is another change in her pictures. The scribbles, instead of spreading without control over the whole sheet of paper, are now more restricted. Occasionally she produces a few isolated lines and, sometimes, gives them a name. At the age of two she created her first clearly recognizable image – a flower (see illustration 5).

ILLUSTRATION 5

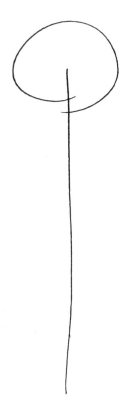

ILLUSTRATION 6

It seems that the ability to draw with realism arises in one of two ways. The first is observation. Tracey watched keenly as her older sister sat drawing or painting. Then she would try and copy the hand and arm movements. Second, the child experiments haphazardly and discovers that some of the lines drawn look similar to things in his or her surroundings and repeats the movements if the result is pleasing. As in Tracey's case, the first truly formal pictures which children create are frequently human figures, although animals and plants are also popular. This picture of her mother, see illustration 6, was made at the age of 30 months.

Humans and animals remain favourites as the child grows older, with plants suffering a decline in popularity and everyday objects becoming increasingly attractive. After examining 1570 drawings by children aged 5–15, Dr Louis Maitland was able to rate the popularity of various subjects as follows:

Utensils and other objects in daily use 41 per cent

Humans   33 per cent

Plants   27 per cent

Houses   25 per cent

Animals   18 per cent

Children under the age of ten, however, were more likely to draw animals (25 per cent) than those aged 11–17 (10 per cent).

The child's first attempts at the human form are very primitive and tentative. Only the head and body may be represented initially, and these are only drawn more completely as the child grows older. The chart below shows the stages at which different parts of the figure are most likely to be included:

ILLUSTRATION 7

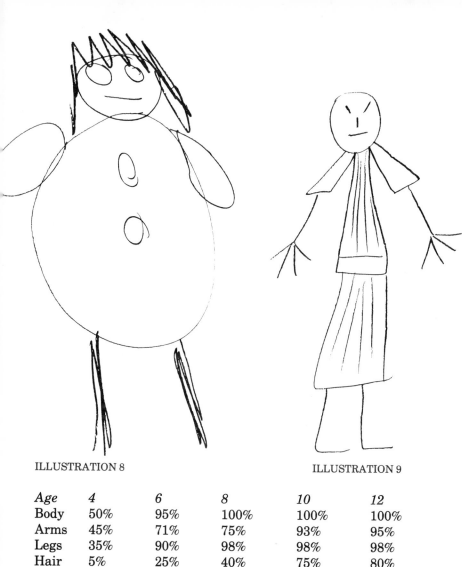

ILLUSTRATION 8   ILLUSTRATION 9

Age	4	6	8	10	12
Body	50%	95%	100%	100%	100%
Arms	45%	71%	75%	93%	95%
Legs	35%	90%	98%	98%	98%
Hair	5%	25%	40%	75%	80%
Clothes	15%	40%	65%	85%	90%

Tracey's human figures became increasingly complete and detailed, as the drawings in illustrations 7–9, at ages 4, 5 and 6, indicate. Human portrayal generally starts out with the full face, adding the profile only in later stages, with different parts of the figure being turned as the child's skill and perception increase. The sequence we have seen most often is – feet; nose; eyes and mouth. This agrees with the observations of some child specialists, but others report the sequence as – feet; arms; body and head. Animals, however, are nearly always drawn in profile from the first and only appear full-face in the pictures of much older children.

Like other six-year-olds, Tracey never represented her own viewpoint in pictures. She would instead produce a drawing which conveyed the most information possible. This is a universal feature of the art of the under-sevens. When asked to draw two bricks standing side by side, for instance, Tracey

ILLUSTRATION 10

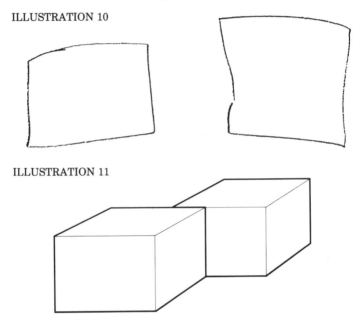

ILLUSTRATION 11

drew the perfectly correct picture shown in illustration 10. However, when we moved the bricks so that one now partially blocked the other, her representation remained unchanged.

One brick now partly conceals the second (see illustration 11). But Tracey, like other children of her age, continues to picture them standing side by side.

Given a cup with the handle turned away from her to draw, Tracey, like most under-sevens, insisted on including the handle although she could not see it (see illustration 12). However, when asked to draw two cups side by side, where

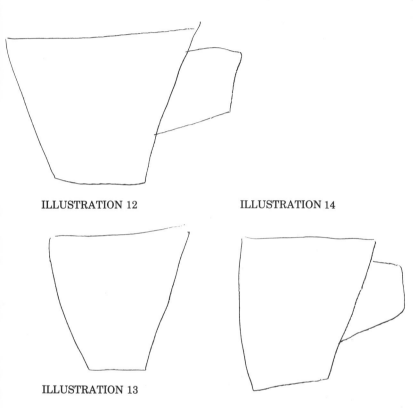

ILLUSTRATION 12   ILLUSTRATION 14

ILLUSTRATION 13

only one handle had been turned away from her, she drew them perfectly accurately (see illustration 13). Investigating this way of representing objects, Dr Paul Light, of the University of Southampton, used a transparent beaker and a solid wooden house. When the house was placed inside the beaker, the under-sevens had no difficulty in drawing it correctly (see illustration 14). However, when the house was placed behind the beaker, it was drawn standing alongside it – even though the child's view of the house was unchanged (see illustration 15).

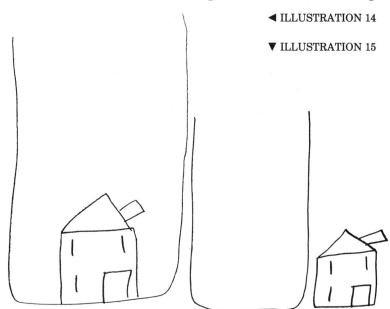

The great Swiss child psychologist Jean Piaget argued that this apparent blindness to reality was explained by the fact that under the age of seven children are unable to depict a particular viewpoint. They seek to draw the most comprehensive view, rather than the view which, through the use of perspective and occlusion (the partial blocking of one part of the image by another), shows a specific aspect of the scene.

Children can only start to represent a particular viewpoint once they have mastered the art of perspective, a skill rarely found below the age of 13. In this respect there are great similarities between children's pictures and primitive drawings, where there is also an emphasis on outline and surface. It is found in Palaeolithic art, as well as that of Bushmen, and Eskimos, Greek vase-painting and the work of the ancient Egyptians. An inability to represent perspective (or a lack of interest in it) persisted well into the Middle Ages and can be seen in the work of early Renaissance artists as well. Unlike these painters, however, most children find it almost impossible to represent movement effectively. While the work of primitive artists is often vital and energetic, the art of a child tends to be static and frozen. Drawing movement convincingly is one of the last skills to be mastered and many never acquire the ability.

The final point we should consider is the use of proportion. As we have seen, distortions of the human figure can indicate how a child feels about that person. Getting the proportions correct is a skill, however, which has to be acquired by practice and experience. One of the most common errors is drawing the head too large. Tracey's pictures, above, are good illustrations of this type of mistake. The probable explanation is that faces are especially fascinating to children who often get the opportunity for seeing them at very close range, and so it is likely that faces will receive far more attention than any other

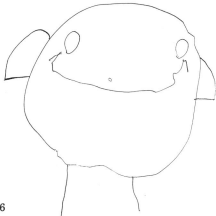

ILLUSTRATION 16

part of the body. Errors of proportion also occur, however, within the features on the face (see illustration 16).

Eyes are sometimes drawn so large in early pictures that they may take up at least half the face, while the mouth is frequently shown as a line extending almost from ear to ear. The nose may be left out or represented by a dot, while ears project like jug handles.

It seems likely that this distortion occurs for two reasons. First, the child tends to emphasize those parts of the face which are especially interesting and significant. Anybody who has watched an infant staring with fascination into his mother's eyes, or – long before he can speak – pursing and puckering his lips to mimic the movements of her mouth will recognize the importance of these particular features to young children. Ears are shown prominently because, in many people, they are a fairly obvious feature of the head. The nose, however, is only of minor interest because it is usually rather small in any case and has, unlike the eyes and mouth, little part to play in silent speech signals. Arms are usually drawn too long, particularly if the child is representing action and needs to make the hands stretch to reach something. Legs, by comparison, are almost always drawn too short, as are fingers and feet.

The second major reason for the mistakes in proportion is that young children find it hard to attend both to details and to the overall picture. They cannot see the image as a whole while concentrating on different aspects of the drawing. When studying your child's pictures for any of the features described in this book, it is essential to keep these factors in mind. Do this by looking for variations of style within established conventions of drawing; for instance, if a young child always misses out hands or arms, this should be seen as a perfectly natural part of their development. If, however, hands and arms are suddenly omitted, their absence probably has another meaning and a deeper psychological significance.

Do not worry if your child takes longer to master certain drawing skills than other children, or than has been suggested here, since children's perceptual and intellectual abilities mature at different rates. Their growth can be likened to an incoming tide: although different parts of the sands are reached at various times, the whole seashore is eventually covered.

Collect and preserve as many of your children's pictures as possible, from the earliest scribbles to their more accomplished later works. These images, so often discarded as of no more than passing interest, are a detailed and revealing pictorial biography. They are both a mirror reflecting the child's outlook and a permanent record of fleeting feelings.

A picture, someone once said, is worth a thousand words. But when it comes to telling the story of childhood, pictures give voice to words that will never be spoken.